THE OPEN UNIVERSITY

Social Sciences: a third level course
Research Methods in Education and
the Social Sciences

Block 3B   Research Design

DE304 Research Methods in Education and the Social Sciences

Central Course Team

Michael Wilson (Chairman)

John Bynner
(Chairman, Production)

Judith Calder
Peter Coxhead
Jeff Evans (on secondment
  from Middlesex Polytechnic)
Martyn Hammersley
Jane Henry (IET)
Fred Lockwood (IET)
Robert Peacock
Roger Sapsford
Keith Stribley (Course Assistant)
Betty Swift
Melanie Bayley (Editor)
Giles Clark (Editor)
Aldwyn Cooper (SCS)
Peter Cox (SCS)
Martyn Haywood (SCS)
Vic Lockwood (BBC)
Ken Patton (BBC)
Tag Taylor (Designer)
Eleanor Thompson (Project Control)

External Assessor
Marie Jahoda CBE
(Emeritus Professor of Social
Psychology, University of Sussex)

Internal Consultants
Christopher Brook
Michael Drake
Judith Greene
Andrew Pollard
Adrian Thomas

External Consultants
Liz Atkins, Medical Research Council
Paul Atkinson, University College, Cardiff
Martin Bulmer, London School of Economics
Wyn Lewis, University of Warwick
Cathie Marsh, University of Cambridge
Peter Martin, University of Manchester
Desmond Nuttall, Middlesex Examining Board
Bram Oppenheim, London School of Economics
Albert Pilliner, University of Edinburgh
David Romney, Laurentian University, Ontario

Acknowledgements

The Course Team are indebted to the following for their assistance: John Murrell and John Bibby for their comments on the draft material; Patrick Miller for preparing the Glossary; David Short and the students who developmentally tested the course; Professor Jim Davis for invaluable help with the survey analysis section; Paul Smith for preparing the course library guide; Michael Levers and Tim Chard for photographic work; Keith Howard for graphic illustrations; Liz Joseph, Cathy Bayntun, Mary Cox, Betty Gregory and Ann Boomer, who were the course secretaries; Pat Coombes and Glenna White who helped with the preparation of drafts for publishing. Many others, both from the Open University and elsewhere, have helped to realize this course – to them our thanks.

The Open University Press
Walton Hall, Milton Keynes
MK7 6AA

First published 1979. Reprinted 1981, 1986.

Copyright © 1979   The Open University

Designed by the Graphic Design Group of the Open University.

Printed in Great Britain by Staples Printers St Albans Limited at The Priory Press.

ISBN 0 335 07423 5

This text forms part of an Open University course. The complete list of the course appears at the end of this text.

For general availability of supporting material referred to in this text, please write to Open University Educational Enterprises Limited, 12 Cofferidge Close, Stony Stratford, Milton Keynes, MK11 1BY, Great Britain.

Further information on Open University courses may be obtained from the Admissions Office, The Open University, P.O. Box 48, Walton Hall, Milton Keynes, MK7 6AB.

1.3

Part 4   Introduction to Applied Sampling
Prepared by Judith Calder for the Course Team

Block 3 Part 4

Contents

Aims

To present the principles of sampling in research on human population, the means of estimating sampling errors, and the different types of sample design.

Study Guide

Work through the correspondence text reading the extracts from Smith (Set Book) as indicated. Then read the article by Hedges, 'Sampling minority populations', which is recommended reading for this Part. To grasp the distinction between the different sampling designs and their effect on the precision of population estimates you will find it valuable to try out the SAMP SCS program.

If you want to go further into the subject of sampling, Moser and Kalton is an excellent basic text. The main theoretical treatment of sampling is in the book by Kish.

Set Reading

SMITH, H. W. (1975) 'Sampling: the search typicality', *Strategies of social research: the methodological imagination*, Ch. 6, pp. 105–20 only.

Recommended Reading

HEDGES, B. (1979) 'Sampling minority populations', in Wilson, M. J. (ed) (1979) *Social and educational research in action: a book of readings*, Ch. 12.

Further Reading

KISH, L. (1965) *Survey sampling*, New York, John Wiley and Sons.

MOSER, C. A. and KALTON, G. (1971) *Survey methods in social investigations,* London, Heinemann.

1   Introduction

... the Minister of Education asked us 'to consider primary education in all its aspects and the transition to secondary education'. (Plowden Report, Vol. 1, para. 1, p. 1)

The enquiry was conducted amongst the parents of a sample of children of certain age-groups in maintained primary schools in England.

The sample design was a stratified random one in two stages with maintained primary schools in England as the primary sampling units. At the second stage ... (Plowden Report, Vol. 2, Annex 1, p. 147)

1.1   The extracts above show the extent of the problem which so often faces researchers. Faced with the vague sort of brief you see above they have to develop the brief to the point where they can specify precisely the population which they are going to study, whether they are going to sample, the way in which they are going to sample, and the methods they are going to employ in gathering their data. In this Part we will be discussing the sampling problems which arise and the decisions which must be taken at each stage in the development of the original research idea to the stage where a specific sample design has been devised.

2   Pre-sampling Problems

Before starting this section read Smith (1975) Ch. 6, 'Sampling: the search for typicality', pp. 105–14.

**Now read
Smith (1975) pp. 105–14**

Defining the Population

2.1   The first step to be taken before the sampling process actually begins is to decide who or what you are going to sample. The population that you as the researcher are interested in will almost certainly differ from the very specific population from which you decide to sample. A useful way of looking at the population a researcher decides to study is suggested in Smith (Set Book). He highlights the difference between the 'working' universe and the 'general' universe. Briefly, the *working universe*, or *working population* as it is often called, is the precisely specified population the researcher is actually going to study. The *general universe* (or *general population*), on the other hand, is the wider population to which the researcher (or other researchers) sees his or her findings as relevant.

**working universe
or population,
general universe
or population**

2.2   This distinction is a very important one as too great a gap between the two can lead to serious bias. A researcher who studied only registered childminders (the working population) should not attempt to draw conclusions about all childminders (the general population), as unregistered childminders are likely to be different in many ways from registered childminders, e.g. minimum standards may not be met. In this sort of situation the researcher must either restrict conclusions to the working population or he must find a way of including unregistered minders in the study.

2.3   Smith mentions two levels of difference between the working population and the general population. The first arises through the operationalization of the general population and is usually unavoidable. Records may be incomplete, parts of the population may be very difficult to access, but such problems can be identified and the effects minimized. When the gaps and omissions look as if they might be serious, then the researcher must think about redefining the working population.

2.4 The second level of difference between the working population and the general population arises through what Smith calls the 'leaps of faith'. With the Plowden study, researchers will almost certainly generalize from that study to children in Scottish schools, or to Wales and Northern Ireland, even though the working population was restricted to schools in England. All the researcher can do to dampen down the possibility of too imaginative a 'leap of faith' is to state, very precisely in the research report, the actual working population, as did the Plowden researchers.

2.5 Once the area of interest has been roughed out, the population is usually described in terms of the units which are included in that population. So for Plowden, though the population associated with primary education could be defined in a number of ways, the researchers defined it in terms of the units (children in maintained schools) which comprise a working population that is easily accessible — accessible in the sense that maintained schools are not only easily identified but there exist central records which make identification *and* contact easy.

Identifying the Population

2.6 In the extract you read at the beginning of this section, Smith discusses the problem of *accessibility* both of samples and of whole populations. As we have seen, a population is only accessible if it can be *identified* and it can only be identified if it is first *defined*. Let us look at what we mean by these terms. There are basically only two rules which must be met if a working population is to be adequately defined: the definition must be *explicit*, and it must be *unambiguous*.

If a researcher said that he wished to study OU Maths graduates, would you consider he had adequately defined his population?

Write your answer, with reasons, here, then read paragraph 2.7 below.

Not quite. All or only honours, or those with certain classes. Also all since OU began? or certain years.

2.7 In fact, it would not be clear exactly whom he wished to study. Would he include in the population all graduates with at least one credit in a maths faculty course? Would he count any interdisciplinary courses with an 'M' in the course number? Or perhaps he would wish to count only post-foundation courses. Notice that in order to answer this question the researcher needs detailed knowledge of the rules and the structure of the organization concerned. After the population has been defined in such a way that it is quite clear to any third party who is and who is not included, the researcher must then check whether the individual members of that population are identifiable. Let us look at this problem by taking another example.

2.8   A number of studies have been carried out within the OU on students who give up their studies before completing the course – these are termed 'drop-outs'. Researchers at the OU define the population of 'drop-outs' quite precisely and unambiguously. They split the 'drop-outs' into two groups: those who dropped out before final registration, and those who dropped out after final registration. The early 'drop-outs' were defined as those who provisionally registered for a course, but did not finally register. The later 'drop-outs' were defined as those who finally registered for a course, but did not sit the exam.

2.9   The major problem then was how to *identify* this population. Students may write in and tell the University when they decide to discontinue their studies on a particular course, but the usual pattern is for them to stop studying, either over a period of time or as a result of a sudden decision, while continuing to receive their correspondence materials. As far as the University knows these students are still studying. Even the non-return of assignments may not be a good indicator as a student may well simply choose not to complete assignments in the middle of the course and then complete all the later ones. Therefore, although the researchers could *define* their population, it was not until after the end of the University year that the population could actually be *identified*.

2.10   Although the population was now defined and identified, permission for *access* still had to be obtained from the University Committee responsible for ensuring that students are not deluged by questionnaires.

2.11   One final problem remained, that of the *level of response*, which continues to be a problem for this population. Because of the delay in being able to identify them, many of the members of this population may have moved, while others no longer have much interest in the University. The usual method of approach by researchers at the OU is by postal questionnaire. Those members of the population who have moved without notifying the University of their new address cannot be contacted, whilst those with a low level of interest may only be willing to respond if a personal approach is made, rather than a rather impersonal approach by correspondence.

2.12   We have been using terms such as 'identify', 'access', 'contact' when talking about the choice of a working population, and indeed, once the theoretical bases for selecting a particular population have been established, practical constraints such as these often result in a redefinition or even a reconceptualization of the working population. In other words the sort of information which is available about a population, whether contact can be made and so on, all affect the final decision about the population.

SAQ 1
Briefly outline the main pre-sampling steps you should go through before deciding finally on any working population.

Why a Sample?

2.13   Before we go any further, you should be quite clear about the distinction between a census and a sample. Briefly, a *census* is an enumeration of a whole population, as we saw in Block 1, whereas a *sample* enquiry uses only part of a population from which certain attributes of the population to which it belongs may be inferred. You should appreciate that the terms 'sample' or 'census' might be used in relation to the same group of individuals depending on the circumstances. If the group is seen only as part of a larger population, then it is a sample and we would do a survey on it, for example, but if the group contains the whole working population, then we would be doing a census. Thus, which term we use is determined by the role we assign to the group, or by the way in which we define the working population.

SAQ 2

If we looked at the distribution of grades that students studying DE304 had been awarded during the course of the year, would we be taking a sample or a census?

2.14   Going back now to our original question, why does a researcher make a decision to sample? First, there is *reduced cost*. Where the same procedures are used for either a sample or a census, or where the cost of collecting the data is high in relation to the total cost, the costs from using only a proportion of the population will be less than using a census. Similarly, there can be *savings in time* as information can be collected and processed more quickly with a sample than with a census. A sample can have *fewer non-sampling errors* than a census. These non-sampling errors would be present in a complete census as well as in a sample, e.g. through faulty recording of information. With a sample survey, for instance, the volume of work is reduced, better trained interviewers can be used, there can be more careful supervision of fieldwork and more sensitive instruments of measurement may be used. By the same argument, a *wider range of topics* can be investigated, in that very complicated subjects (such as family expenditure) or sensitive topics (such as family planning) can be investigated by using specially selected and trained interviewers to collect the information.

non-sampling error

2.15   Given these advantages, why should anyone ever choose to use a census based on a complete enumeration? What drawbacks are there? The main problem is *sampling error*. Samples are, by definition, only part of the parent population, and therefore, particularly with a human population, cannot have exactly the same characteristics as that population. With what is called a *'probability sample'* (see paragraphs 3.17 and 3.18 below), however, we can calculate an estimate, from the sample, of the results that would have been obtained from a complete enumeration. The *difference* between the sample result and the one which would have been obtained from a complete enumeration taken with the same methods of collection and the same care as the sample, is called the *sampling error*. This should not be confused with the other sorts of error common to sample surveys and censuses which we shall be looking at in Block 4 – *measurement error*; nor should it be confused with systematic errors or *biases*, e.g. the population list contains only women or too many old people, etc.

sampling error

measurement error, bias

2.16   Sampling errors are those random or chance fluctuations from population values that we may expect to find as a result of not covering the whole population in any one sample. We say that the smaller the sampling error is for a particular sample estimate, the higher the *precision* of the sample. Obviously if all the population are included, as in a census, then we reach a limit of maximum precision in which sampling errors are zero. Similarly the smallest sample possible containing only one population member has maximum sampling error associated with it and has minimal precision. Note the distinction between the precision of a sample and its *accuracy*. Accuracy refers to all the errors and biases in a particular sample, not just those connected with probability (or random) sampling.

precision

accuracy

SAQ 3

Suppose you wish to select a sample of teachers at a particular point in time. You first need to establish a working population. Give examples of factors you might wish to use to limit the population in defining your working population and outline briefly the problems you might expect with the remaining pre-sampling steps.

3 The Basic Choice

Before you begin this section read Smith (1975) Ch. 6, 'Sampling: the search for typicality', pp. 114–20, as far as 'simple random sampling'.

Now read Smith (1975) pp. 114–20

3.1 There are two important aspects of sample design:

(a) *Selection:* the different rules and procedures for choosing which members (elements) of the population are to form the sample.

selection

(b) *Estimation:* the process by which estimates of population values are obtained from the sample.

estimation

As Smith points out, there are two generic types of samples: *purposive* and *probability* (also referred to as 'random' (Moser and Kalton, 1971)). Both types of sample differ from each other with respect to the selection aspect *and* the estimation aspect.

3.2 Taking the selection aspect first: a *probability sample* is defined as a sample in which all members of the population have a *known chance* of selection. In addition, no member is assured of selection, and no member is excluded from selection. With a *non-probability or purposive sample* at least one of these three conditions will not be met, that is, the chance of selection is unknown, or some members will be assured of selection, or some members will be excluded from selection.

probability or random sample

non-probability or purposive sample

3.3 With respect to the estimation aspect, *only with probability samples can statistically valid estimates be produced* (i.e. estimates from which sampling errors can be calculated). Although estimates can be and are produced for purposive samples, there is no statistically valid way of measuring the sampling error. Therefore, any estimates produced have to be taken on trust. One simple check which can be carried out is to check the representativeness of the sample by comparing the distribution of the main characteristics in the sample with those of the population (where known).

Non-probability or Purposive Sampling

3.4 Other things being equal, probability samples should normally be used. However, conditions may be such that a probability sample is either not feasible or is not the best sort of sample for meeting the research objectives in a particular situation. In any research project, there is a certain sequence of activities the researcher must follow: namely, to identify, select and contact the sample; interview, test or observe the sample; and collate and analyse the findings. Problems can arise at any of these stages and can affect the researcher's decision about the most appropriate types of sample to use.

3.5 Problems in *identifying* members of the population in which the researcher is interested can arise where, for example, they are engaged in illegal activities (such as drug-taking). Social pressures may make identification of certain groups difficult. For instance, identification of people who are illiterate, or of couples who are unmarried, can present considerable difficulties for researchers. Even where these difficulties are not present, there can be problems of *contacting* members of a specific population. For instance a study of a class of students ten years after graduation would present many problems at this stage.

3.6 In 'Sampling minority populations' Hedges (1979) describes a number of ways of solving problems of this kind. One solution is to use a *snowball sample*. Briefly this is a method of building up a sample by starting with a small base of informants, and getting from them the names and addresses of other people who fall into the same group, or share the same characteristics. The principle is very much that of a chain letter. With this method, it is obviously impossible to assign any probability of selection to the informants.

snowball sample

3.7 For other types of studies, the problem may not be so much one of identification or contact, but of co-operation. The research may well involve lengthy tests or the use of complex equipment; there may be extended interviews on difficult or esoteric subjects; the researcher may wish to observe the subjects over a period of time. In situations where such problems are likely to occur, the researcher may well feel that a *volunteer sample* best meets his or her requirements. Such samples, where subjects or informants 'volunteer' themselves are often used in medicine and psychology. (This was essentially the method used in the Milgram research (1963) described in Part 1, with the additional feature that those 'volunteers' were paid.) A piece of research currently being carried out in the OU is using such a method. Students of the T100 foundation course are participating in a national 'noise' survey as part of their study. Each student has been issued with a noise meter which they use for taking measurements of noise in different parts of their own locality. These measurements are fed back to Walton Hall to be transferred to a national map. Over a period of time, the coverage should be quite extensive. Compare this solution with the alternative of selecting a sample of areas and finding people who were both willing and able to use expensive and fairly delicate machines.

volunteer sample

Block 3, Part 1, section 1

3.8 Another solution which can be used to deal with some of the problems mentioned above is to use a *case study* approach. This type of approach will be discussed in relation to ethnographic research in the next Part of this Block. In general terms, it can involve the choice of a 'typical' unit, a 'deviant' unit, or merely a convenient unit. If the unit selected is a large community there is of course no reason why a probability sample of people within that community cannot be selected. For instance, Wilmott and Young (1960) in their study, *Family and class in a London suburb,* used this approach.

case study
Block 3, Part 5, para. 3.7

3.9 The major form of non-probability sample used by commercial organizations for interview surveys is *quota sampling*. Kish describes quota sampling as,

quota sampling

> Sizes of subclasses in the population are estimated, based on Census or other data. Quotas of desired numbers of sample cases are computed proportionally to the population subclasses. The sample quotas are divided among the interviewers, who then do their best to find persons who fit the restrictions of their quota controls. (Kish, 1965, p. 563)

3.10 The reasons for using quota sampling tend to be different *in nature* from the reasons for using other forms of non-probability sampling we have discussed. They can obviously be used where there is no population list available, but even where a list is available they are often used to reduce *costs*. Where a probability sample of individuals is selected for an interview survey, the interviewer may well have to call back a number of times before finding that person at home (a limit of four calls is usually imposed because the law of diminishing returns usually sets in at this point – the cost of getting the interview is becoming prohibitive). Even if the person is at home at the first call, the common procedure is to make an appointment to interview that person at a convenient time. Compare the cost of this sort of approach with that of stopping someone in the street (as in some quota samples).

3.11   You should be aware, however, that there is a certain amount of controversy over the precise level of saving here. Moser and Kalton (1971), for example, argue that:

> A true cost comparison is made not in terms of cost per interview, but rather in terms of the cost of a survey for a prescribed level of precision. While no accurate comparisons are available, it has been suggested that, because callbacks are avoided and because there is no need to travel all over a town to track down pre-selected respondents, a quota interview costs on average only half or a third as much as a random interview; but for most surveys it is likely that much, if not all, of this apparent saving would disappear if the proper cost comparisons were made. (Moser and Kalton, 1971, p. 134)

3.12   One of the main problems with quota samples is that they are prone to certain biases: for instance interviews in a shopping centre during the week would tend to miss working women and men; interviews near a railway station might be biased towards those who use that form of transport, and so on.

3.13   There are circumstances, however, when a quota sample is the only possibility. This is where *time* is of crucial importance. During election time for example, commercial firms can achieve a 'turnaround' time of three days, i.e. from asking people their voting intentions to publishing the results.

3.14   There are many other variations of non-probability samples. The factors affecting the researchers' decision to use them will usually be similar to the ones discussed above. It should be pointed out that there is no one term in common use to describe what we have been calling non-probability samples. Other terms most commonly used are *judgement sampling, haphazard sampling* and, as in Smith, *purposive sampling*.

3.15   Although probability sampling and non-probability or purposive samples are different generically, it is possible to improve non-probability samples by combining the two approaches. This can best be explained by looking at two different types of non-probability sample. With quota sampling, for example, although the actual individuals in the sample are purposively selected, the geographical areas the interviewers go to can be, and in fact usually are, selected using a probability method (see multi-stage cluster sampling, section 6, paragraphs 6.7–6.9). Because of the inclusion of this probability element, **paras 6.7–6.9** researchers sometimes argue that they are justified in calculating an estimate of what the sampling error would have been had it been a complete probability sample. They also maintain that any quota sample *is* one of the possible samples that would have been obtained by random methods. There is no way of knowing, however, how reliable are estimates from such a sample.

3.16   The reverse process can happen with the case study type of sample, where the 'case' is a large unit such as a town, factory or school. Here, although the initial selection of the 'case' is purposive, the selection of individuals or units from within it could use a probability design. The advantage of this approach is that the 'case' can be considered to be the working population and valid estimates of the sampling error can be calculated. For generalizations outside the 'case' no valid figure for the sampling error could be attached to any estimates.

SAQ 4

Suppose researchers at the OU wish to study self-help groups and similar kinds of informal student study networks. Assume that the researchers wish to find out both what kind of networks there are and how they developed, and they also wish to get some idea about the number of students involved in them.

Working on the basis that resources are fairly limited (say two people full-time for six months) would you recommend that they use a probability or non-probability type of sample? Outline (briefly) your reasons.

Probability or Random Sampling

3.17 All samples aim to a certain extent for representativeness at their selection stage. As we have already pointed out, however, there is only *one* type of sampling from which statistically valid estimates can be produced, and that is *probability or random* sampling. We can define this as any method of sampling in which *every element in the population has a known, non-zero, probability of selection* (Kish, 1965). This means simply that we should know what the probability of selection is for every person in the defined population, and that *everyone* should have a chance of being selected.

3.18 Before the selection for a probability sample can take place, it is necessary to identify the individual members of the population in some way. This is normally done either by constructing, or by getting access to, a sampling frame. The term 'frame' is used when we talk of the enumeration of the population for sampling purposes: for instance, for any studies of current OU students, a good sampling frame would be the student record file held on the central computer.

SAQ 5

A researcher tells you that she intends to select a probability sample of 1 in 10 students attending any OU study centre on a specified evening. Is she correct in calling it a probability sample? Note down the reasons for your answer.

Sampling Frames

3.19 A *sampling frame* can be anything through which all the population elements are identified. As we have seen it can be a computer file, but it could be a simple list, or it may take forms such as a map or set of maps. Nor need a frame be held in one central place, although it is obviously easier to use if it is. For instance, records of building-site workers may only be available on each site rather than in a central office. Whatever format the frame takes, there are certain checks which need to be made before you decide whether it can be used for sampling purposes. Consider the following example.

sampling frame

3.20 *Example 1* We want to select a sample of 50 patients over the age of 25 in a local hospital. We know that approximately 40% of the 200 patients are aged 25 or under. The only frame available, the hospital files, can only be made available for sampling purposes for a short time and therefore we cannot sort out the ineligibles before sampling. Before we select the sample we should first check:

(a) *Does the sample size need adjusting?* (This applies only if systematic selection is used: see paragraphs 4.7 to 4.14.) The frame contains 200 names of whom 120 form our working population (60% of 200). If we select a sample of

paras 4.7–4.14

only 50 from the whole population, then we would expect only 60% (i.e. 30) to be over the age of 25 and therefore eligible for our study. We therefore have to allow for this by adjusting the sample size upwards so that we end up with 50 patients over the age of 25. That is, we need $\frac{200}{120} \times 50 = 83.3$, i.e. 84 individuals.

(b) *Extent of coverage*   Are all groups of patients included in the set of files we want to use? (E.g. the geriatric unit might keep its own files.)

(c) *Completeness of the frame*   Are the records for all the patients there or are some missing, being used by doctors or nurses or being updated?

(d) *Amount and quality of auxiliary information*   Is the date of birth given, or is the age of the patient written in? If the latter, has it been updated, or is it the age on entry to the hospital? This check is particularly important for what are called 'stratified samples' as we shall see later (section 5).

(e) *Duplication*   Are people included more than once in the frame?

4   The Basic Design: Simple Random Sampling

4.1   We saw in section 3 that there were two principal aspects to sampling – selection and estimation. It is the combination of the procedures which are used for each of these aspects which we call the *sample design*. The simplest and most basic kind of sample design is the *simple random sample* (srs) in which all the elements in the population have the same known probability of appearing in the sample.

simple random sample

4.2   In the standard texts on sampling, two types of simple random sample are identified, namely simple random sampling *with replacement* and simple random sampling *without replacement*. In sampling *with replacement* once an element has been selected it is put back into the population and stands the same chance of being reselected. *Theoretically* it would be possible although highly unlikely for a sample of size *n* to be composed of one element selected *n* times! In sampling *without replacement*, once an element has been selected, it is not put back into the population and therefore it can only be selected once. In practice, sampling *with* replacement is rarely appropriate or feasible, and, certainly in education and the social sciences, it is rarely, if ever, used. Consequently the rest of this unit will refer only to sampling without replacement.

simple random sample with replacement

simple random sample without replacement

4.3   Selecting a sample by the random process that probability sampling requires can present technical difficulties. Texts on sampling often use the analogy of selecting balls from urns or of shuffling numbers in a hat, in much the same fashion as a raffle ticket is chosen. In practice a random number table, or the pseudo-random scheme known as systematic selection is generally used.

Random Selection

4.4   For smaller samples, *random numbers* are used. These are tables of numbers which are generated at random by a computer. In such a table all numbers appear the same number of times overall – so each one has the same probability of being included in any sample consisting of a list of consecutive numbers (see Table 1).

random numbers

Table 1   1000 random digits

00	49487	52802	28667	62058	87822	14704	18519	17889	45869	14454
01	29480	91539	46317	84803	86056	62812	33584	70391	77749	64906
02	25252	97738	23901	11106	86864	55808	22557	23214	15021	54268
03	02431	42193	96960	19620	29188	05863	92900	06836	13433	21709
04	69414	89353	70724	67893	23218	72452	03095	68333	13751	37260
05	77286	35179	92042	67581	67673	68374	71115	98166	43352	06414
06	52852	11444	71868	34534	69124	02760	06406	95234	87995	78560
07	98740	98054	30195	09891	18453	79464	01156	95522	06884	55073
08	85022	58736	12138	35146	62085	36170	25433	80787	96496	40579
09	17778	03840	21636	56269	08149	19001	67367	13138	02400	89515
10	81833	93449	57781	94621	90998	37561	59688	93299	27726	82167
11	63789	54958	33167	10909	40343	81023	61590	44474	39810	10305
12	61840	81740	60986	12498	71546	42249	13812	59902	27864	21809
13	42243	10153	20891	90883	15782	98167	86837	99166	92143	82441
14	45236	09129	58031	12260	01278	14404	40969	33419	14188	69557
15	40338	42477	78804	36272	72053	07958	67158	60979	79891	92409
16	54040	71253	88789	98203	54999	96564	00789	68879	47134	83941
17	49158	20908	44859	29089	76130	51442	34453	98590	37353	61137
18	80958	03808	83655	18415	96563	43582	82207	53322	30419	64435
19	07636	04876	61063	57571	69434	14965	20911	73162	33576	52839

Source: The RAND Corporation, 1955

4.5   To use such a table to obtain a sample from a specified population sampling frame we use the following procedure:

(a)   Determine the number of digits in the population size, N: for example, if $N = 6000$, then we have 4 digits.

(b)   Number the population elements using the appropriate number of digits: for example, for $N = 6000$ number the elements from 0001 to 6000.

(c)   Select the columns to be used from the table of random numbers: for example, for four digits, use four columns.

(d)   Mark off the number of random numbers equal to the required sample size (n); the members of the population bearing these numbers form the sample. If the same number appears more than once, treat it as a blank. Similarly any number greater than N should be treated as a blank.

4.6   Let us see how this works in practice, using the random number table (Table 1). We want to select a sample of $n = 100$ from a population of $N = 6000$. Since there are 4 digits in the number 6000 we use the first four columns of Table 1. (Note that in Table 1 the rows are numbered from 00 to 19; the columns are not numbered, but are presented in groups of five. We shall start off with the first four digits in the first group of five.) We check off the following 4 digit numbers:

4948 ✓

2948 ✓

2525 ✓

0243 ✓

6941 X   (treated as a blank since 6941 > 6000)

7728 X   (treated as a blank since 7728 > 6000)

5285 ✓

and so on, until we have a hundred selections less than or equal to 6000. Having got to the bottom figure 0763 in row 19, we could follow it by 7528 in row 00 using columns 5–8, or more conveniently by 5280 in row 00 using columns 6–9. From the point of view of randomness, it does not matter which we do since the tables have been generated and tested by procedures which ensure that a sample will always be random if a systematic method of selecting from the table is used. The next time we use the table, we would start at the number following the last one previously selected. Some people work along rows, rather than down columns; either method is quite acceptable.

SAQ 6

From the table in Appendix A, select 10 institutions using random selection. Take your random numbers from Table 1, starting from row 07.

Systematic Selection

4.7   Suppose you wanted to carry out an investigation in a factory employing 800 people and you had calculated you needed a sample of about 200. Consider the problem which would arise when you actually started selecting your sample. Would, in fact, random selection as just outlined be the quickest or most efficient method you could use, or is there another approach which would better meet the problem?

4.8   The problem arises because we are dealing with a large population and because we want a relatively large sample. In the situation outlined above, the simplest and quickest solution would be to take the existing frame and go through it selecting every 4th person – in other words to sample *systematically*.

4.9   The calculation for this is as follows: we want a sample of size $n = 200$ from a population of size $N = 800$; therefore the *sampling fraction* (designated f) is:

sampling fraction

$$f = \frac{n}{N} = \frac{200}{800} = \frac{1}{4}$$

The interval between each individual who will be selected is the *sampling interval* (designated k); this is calculated as follows:

sampling interval

$$k = \frac{N}{n} = 4$$

To start the selection process, one should select a digit between 1 and 4 inclusive from a random number table (say 4), and then take the following individuals: $4 + 4 = 8$th, $+ 4 = 12$th, $+ 4 = 16$th . . . and so on.

4.10   Such a procedure is called *systematic sampling*. Unless there is reason to believe otherwise, a systematic sample is usually treated as a simple random sample when it comes to the statistical analysis.

systematic sampling

Advantages and Disadvantages of Systematic Sampling

4.11   The major disadvantages relate to the composition of the frame. When systematic selection is used, there may exist a *periodic cycle* in the frame which could well bias the sample. Examples where such a periodic style exist are not hard to imagine. Suppose that within a school all classes were of size 30, 15 girls and 15 boys, with the girls always listed first. Then a sampling interval of 30, or any integral multiple of 30, would give us a sample of one sex only.

periodic cycle

Figure 1   Periodic cycle

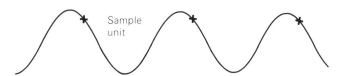

4.12   In such a case it is essential to randomize the order of the list before beginning the sampling. On the other hand when we come to '*stratification*' we shall see that often built-in ordering in a list can be exploited to our advantage.

stratification
paras 5.1–5.15

SAQ 7

From the table in Appendix A, select a sample of 10 institutions, using systematic selection. Compare this sample with the one you obtained for SAQ 6 using random selection, and comment (briefly) on differences between the two samples arising from any inbuilt ordering within the frame.

(*Note* Your random start should be 04, the next 2 digit number in Table 1, the random number table.)

4.13 Systematic sampling is quick and easy to operate, while at the same time it is a simple matter to check for clerical errors. This is particularly important when sampling takes place in the field. For example, it is much easier to select every kth sack in a shed, every kth plant in a row or, as in the 1966 Sample Census, every 10th person in an institution, than to try to cope with random numbers on the spot.

4.14 Another type of situation where systematic sampling is particularly useful is when a frame of the population does not exist at the time of the selection, i.e. where the units of population cannot be known in advance of selection; for example, when sampling admissions to hospitals. Here, the sampling interval k would be calculated by estimating N, the size of the population (say admissions over 7 days) by looking at admissions over previous weeks.

Standard Errors

(Read this section very carefully. You will find sampling much easier to cope with if you understand the discussion in this section.)

4.15 Given that we have actually organized our sampling frame, selected a simple random sample, and got some sample results, how do we decide how accurate the sample results are? For simplicity let's look at a population of only 12 individuals. In Table 2 we show the incomes of the members of the population.

Table 2   Incomes of a hypothetical population of twelve individuals

Individual	Income (£)
A	1 300
B	6 300
C	3 100
D	2 000
E	3 600
F	2 200
G	1 800
H	2 700
I	1 500
J	900
K	4 800
L	1 900
Total income	32 100
Average income	2 675

Source: Hansen, Hurwitz and Madow, 1953, p. 13

4.16 Now the mean income of the people in *any sample* is an *estimate* of the mean income of the *population* we are investigating. If we look at all the possible samples of size 7 (say) that can be drawn from the population (792 in all), we will be able to see how precise any one sample estimate is. Moreover, we can calculate what error, 'on average', we can expect from a single sample. Figure 2 shows the

Figure 2   Distribution of the estimates of average income for all the possible samples of size 7 (792 in all) from the population in Table 2

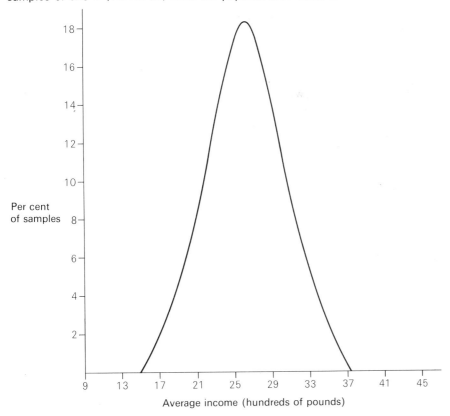

Average income (hundreds of pounds)

distribution or spread of the estimates of average incomes for all the possible samples of size 7 drawn from the population given in Table 2.

You can see that the shape of the curve is very similar to that of a *normal distribution*. The normal distribution has some very useful features, not least of which is that a fixed percentage of cases fall into the ranges measured by the standard deviations (see Figure 3).

normal distribution

Figure 3   A normally distributed set of measurements showing the proportion of measurements lying within the ranges measured by the standard deviations

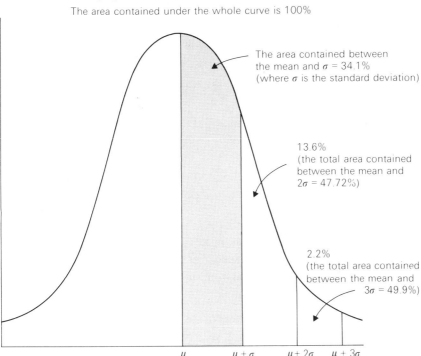

The area contained under the whole curve is 100%

The area contained between the mean and σ = 34.1% (where σ is the standard deviation)

13.6% (the total area contained between the mean and 2σ = 47.72%)

2.2% (the total area contained between the mean and 3σ = 49.9%)

μ $\mu + \sigma$ $\mu + 2\sigma$ $\mu + 3\sigma$

4.17   In other words, *with a normally distributed set of measurements, approximately 68% of all measurements lie within plus or minus one standard deviation from the mean, and approximately 95% lie within two standard deviations.*

4.18   When the measurements are sample estimates of a population value, e.g. the mean income as in our example, we use the term *standard error* (denoted by $s_{\bar{x}}$) rather than *standard deviation* (denoted by σ). So whenever you see the term standard error used, you will know that the distribution of *sample estimates* is being referred to. The outcome of this is that with sample estimates, as for any other measurements which have a normal distribution, we can say what percentage of the estimates will fall within a specific range.

**standard error,
standard deviation,
sample estimate**

4.19   This still leaves us with the problem of how to calculate this range – that is, how do we calculate the standard error (i.e. standard deviation of the distribution of sample estimates) without getting estimates from all possible samples of size n. Obviously if you were able to get information about all possible samples, you would also be able to calculate the population figure in which you were interested and would therefore not need to estimate it from a sample. It can be shown from sampling theory that for a simple random sample (without replacement) of n elements, drawn from a population of N elements, the standard deviation of the distribution of all possible means or *standard error of the mean* is given by:

$$s_{\bar{x}} = (\sqrt{(1-f)}) \frac{\sigma}{\sqrt{n}}$$

where, f is the sampling fraction, and equals $\dfrac{n}{N}$,

and σ is the standard deviation of the population from which the sample is drawn. The above formula reduces to:

$$s_{\bar{x}} = \frac{\sigma}{\sqrt{n}}$$

in the typical case where f is a very small fraction, i.e. less than $1/10$ of the population.

4.20   However, in practice, we do not normally know what σ, the standard deviation of the particular characteristic we are measuring, is for the population. Fortunately, just as we get an estimate of the population mean from one sample, so we can use an estimate of the standard deviation from one sample. To differentiate between the actual figure and the estimate, and to make it quite clear to others that we are using estimates, we use a different notation (although the formula itself remains the same). We now write,

$$s_{\bar{x}} = \sqrt{(1-f)} \frac{s}{\sqrt{n}}$$

(remember, if f is small, you can ignore $\sqrt{(1-f)}$)
where,

$$s = \sqrt{\frac{\Sigma(X_i - \bar{X})^2}{n-1}}$$

Block 2, Part 4, para. 5.17

In other words, the estimate of the standard deviation of the means of all samples of size n, is denoted by $s_{\bar{x}}$, the standard error of the mean of one sample of size n. Similarly the *estimate* of the standard deviation for the population from which the sample is drawn is denoted by s, the standard deviation of the sample.

Note   In this case we are using the symbol s for the sample estimate of the population standard deviation. In Block 2 (Part 4, paragraphs 5.11 to 23) we used it for the standard deviation of the sample itself, i.e.

$$s = \sqrt{\frac{\Sigma(X_i - \bar{X})^2}{n}}$$

This 'double' usage of s is common in statistical literature; for samples greater than 30 it makes no effective difference which formula for s is used.

4.21 By the same argument, we can also use an estimate for calculating the *standard error of a proportion* p. (The proportion p is merely the proportion of the sample possessing the attribute being measured, while q is the proportion which does not possess that attribute, so $p + q = 1$.) Namely,

standard error of a proportion p

$$s_p = (1 - f) \sqrt{\frac{pq}{n}} \simeq \sqrt{\frac{pq}{n}} \text{ for small } f$$

Assume that in a sample of 400 students selected from a course with 4800 students enrolled, the number answering 'yes' to a particular question was 60. What is the (estimate of the) standard error of p?

Make a note of your calculations and your answer here, then compare them with those in paragraph 4.22 below.

$$S_p = (1 - b)\sqrt{\frac{pq}{n}} \qquad b = \frac{400}{4800} = \frac{1}{12}.$$

$$= \sqrt{\frac{pq}{n}}$$

$$\simeq ?$$

$$= \sqrt{\frac{\cdot 15 \times \cdot 85}{400}}$$

$$= 0.0178.$$

$$\text{or } 1.78\%$$

4.22 The sample proportion (p) answering 'yes' is $\frac{60}{400} = 0.15$ or 15%.

Now, $p + q = 1$, so, $q = 1.00 - 0.15 = 0.85$.

As $f = \frac{400}{4800} = \frac{1}{12}$ it can safely be ignored.

The standard error is:

$$s_p = \sqrt{\frac{0.15 \times 0.85}{400}}$$

$$= \sqrt{\frac{0.1275}{400}}$$

$$= \sqrt{0.00031875}$$

$$= 0.0179$$

$$= 1.79 \times \frac{1}{100}$$

$$= 1.79\%$$

(*Note* If you had difficulty with these calculations, you should consult the Developmental and Diagnostic Booklet, or your tutor.)

4.23 In practice, this formula is used quite a lot, as much research, particularly surveys, often present the results in the form of percentages. With the above formula it is very easy to calculate the standard error of a sample proportion.

SAQ 8
From the sample you obtained using systematic selection, calculate the sample estimate of the mean size of UK institutions, and then calculate the standard error of that estimate using the formula in paragraph 4.20.

4.24 Having calculated the standard error for your sample percentage, although you cannot say exactly where on the distribution of all possible samples of that size your sample estimate lies, you *are* now in a position to state *how likely* it is that the actual figure being estimated lies within a specified range. Remember that we said earlier that with a normal distribution, 68% of the measurements would lie within a range of one standard deviation either side of the estimate. (You may wish to refresh your memory by looking at Figure 3.) In sampling terms we can say that 68% of all the possible samples of size *n* would lie within a range of plus or minus one standard error from the estimate; this range is called a *confidence interval*. We are confident that our estimate would come within this range 68 times out of 100, in other words our *level of confidence* would be 68%. In the same way, if we want a 95% level of confidence (the usual level for surveys), we take the *range* given by ±2 standard errors. Your conclusion about the percentage given in the example in paragraph 4.22 above, would therefore read:

confidence interval

level of confidence

'Our estimate of the proportion of students in the population answering "yes" to this question at the 68% level of confidence is 15% ± 1.79%'

or

'Our estimate of the proportion of students in the population answering "yes" to this question at the 95% level of confidence is 15% ± 3.58%'
depending on what level of confidence you decided you wanted for your estimates.

Sample Size

4.25 How does the researcher know the *size* of a sample he or she should select? You might begin by thinking about the effects on the distribution of estimates from larger and smaller samples. Look at Figure 4. Here you can see the results cluster more closely around the mean as the size of the sample increases.

4.26 For a given range of incomes, say £2100–£3100 a much higher proportion of samples of size 24 fall within it than do samples of size 6. In other words, the larger the sample, the smaller the error range. You can see how this works if you look at the error formulae from paragraphs 4.19 and 4.21, i.e.:

$$s_{\bar{x}} = \frac{s}{\sqrt{n}}$$

and

$$s_p = \sqrt{\frac{pq}{n}}$$

Figure 4   Distribution of estimates of average income from samples of various sizes drawn from a population of 12 000 000 individuals with 1 000 000 having each of the incomes given in Table 2

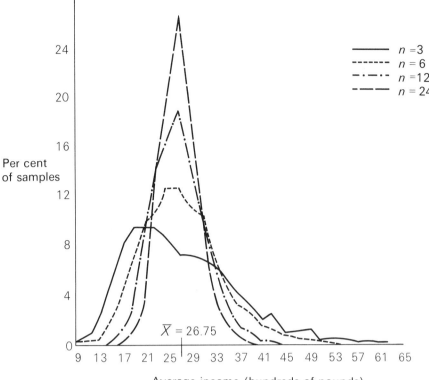

Average income (hundreds of pounds)

Source: Hansen, Hurwitz and Madow, 1953, p. 28

4.27   You will see that the denominator is $\sqrt{n}$ where n is the size of the sample. Therefore the larger n is, the smaller the standard error and the greater the precision. Note the use of the term precision here rather than accuracy. As we saw earlier, *accuracy* refers to all errors and includes the effects of non-sampling errors, whereas *precision* refers only to the size of the deviation of the sample estimate from the population value of the mean (paragraph 2.16 above). Make sure you understand the discussion here, because people often make the mistake of assuming that precision depends on the size of the sample relative to the population. A common trap is for people to ask, 'Is a 10% sample large enough?'. In fact as the formulae above show for all but very small populations (i.e. relatively large f) the crucial factor is *sample size*.

para. 2.16

4.28   The researcher has to decide what level of precision he or she wants for the sample, and sets a value for $s_{\bar{x}}$ or s_p accordingly. Supposing we decided that we want 95% of our sample estimates to fall within 5% of the population value. This gives us $s_p = 2.5\%$ ($2 \times s_p$ gives a 95% confidence interval). To calculate n for a given level of error s_p, we also need information about the proportion p. However $p \times q$ varies only slightly between $p = 0.2$ and $p = 0.8$.

Test this for yourself by completing the following table.

p	0.1	0.2	0.3	0.4	0.5	0.6	0.7	0.8	0.9
q	0.9	0.8	0.7	0.6	0.5	0.4	0.3	0.2	0.1
$p \times q$	0.09	0.16	·21	·24	·25	·24	·21	·16	·09

4.29 As you can see, $p \times q$ varies from a minimum of 0.09, when $p = 0.1$ and $q = 0.09$, to a maximum of 0.25, where $p = 0.5$ and $q = 0.5$. Now, when $p \times q$ is at a maximum, n, the required sample size will be at maximum for any given size of standard error (s_p); this is the 'worst possible' situation. In the absence of other information then, the sample size for $p = 0.5$ can safely be taken. So, for instance, if we wanted to calculate the sample size which would give us a standard error (s_p) no greater than $2\frac{1}{2}\%$, we would use the formula as follows. We have:

$$n = \frac{pq}{s_p^2}(1 - f)^2$$

Assuming the 'worst situation', $p = 0.5$, $q = 0.5$ and that we want $s_p = 2.5\%$ and supposing also that f is small enough to ignore (i.e. less than 1/10), then

$$n = \frac{0.5 \times 0.5}{\left(\frac{2.5}{100}\right)^2}$$

$$= \frac{0.25}{(0.025)^2}$$

$$= \frac{0.25}{0.000625}$$

$$= 400$$

4.30 We have seen that we vary the sample size n to achieve the level of precision required. The decision about what level of precision is required is *not* a question which can be answered by sampling theory and must be decided by the researcher in the light of the overall research objectives. In the end, the question reduces to a trade-off between precision and cost. For instance to aim at a standard error of 2% rather than $2\frac{1}{2}\%$ can mean an increase in the sample size from 400 to 625. The question is whether the improvement in precision is worth the extra cost associated with the larger sample.

SAQ 9

Say the size of your working population is $N = 10\,000$ and you can only afford a sample of size $n = 40$. What would be the size of the standard error for any of your sample percentages in the worst possible case?

4.31 The question of sample size is closely related to the researcher's plans for analysis (see Block 6). If different sub-groups in the population are going to be looked at separately, the sample must be big enough to achieve the required precision for the estimates of the major variables *for each sub-group*. You therefore have to calculate the required sample size for each of the sub-groups you are going to study, and the final sample size will be the *sum* of these 'sub-samples'.

4.32 One feature of surveys which often adds considerably to the sample size is the allowance for *non-response*. It is no good carefully calculating the minimum sample of individuals needed for your study and then finding you are 40% short because only 60% have co-operated. If you are sampling inanimate objects, then there will be no problem, but if you are dependent on the co-operation of anyone (either for access or responsiveness), then your calculated sample size must allow for non-response. If similar types of study have already been carried out, then you can get an estimate of the likely level of non-response, but if you are investigating a new area, or using a new kind of approach, then you will have to seek guidance about the level of response you should assume.

4.33 The final factor which affects sample size is the sample design you use. Up until now, we have been assuming a simple random sample. In the following sections of this unit, we will be looking at the major types of alternative design available, and their effect on the precision of the sample, and consequently on the sample size.

5 Stratified Sampling

5.1 Although the precision of a sample can be increased by increasing its size, this can also increase costs. One way of reducing the standard error without increasing the sample size is by using prior information to increase precision in sample estimates.

Proportionate Stratification

5.2 Suppose you have a population of 12 people – 8 men and 4 women – and you wish to select a sample of 6. You could select a simple random sample, or you could use the information you have about the population and select 4 men and 2 women. In other words, instead of selecting 1 in 2 from the whole population, you can select 1 in 2 units from each group, or *stratum*, separately. You would intuitively expect a better estimate from this sort of sample because you can ensure that you get the right proportion of each sex in the sample, and there is no risk, as with a simple random sample, of getting a 'wild' sample such as 6 men. In other words, you have eliminated a whole range of possible sampling errors – all those for samples which differ from the population with respect to sex ratio. Let us look now at a rather more realistic example.

stratum

5.3 *Example 2*   Suppose we want to select a sample of 400 school leavers from a population of 6000 school leavers in a Local Authority area to see what sort of jobs or what sort of further education they had started on. We feel that a major variable which could affect their choice is the age at which they left school. To get a proportionate stratified sample, we would select 1 in 15 (i.e. $\frac{400}{6000}$) of those who left at 16, 17 and 18 or over. In other words we would take the same percentage of the sample from each stratum that we find in the population (see Table 3).

Table 3

Stratum (school leaving age)	Population size	Percentage of total in each stratum	Sample size	Sampling fraction (*f*)
		Proportionate stratified sample		
16	2 730	45·5	182	1/15
17	1 950	32·5	130	1/15
18 and over	1 320	22	88	1/15
Total	6 000	100	400	1/15

5.4 In this example the school leaving age is the *stratifying factor* and it was broken into three *strata*. In effect a separate sample is selected for each stratum. Because the proportion of the sample which is taken from each stratum is the same as the proportion of the total population which is in that stratum, this type of stratification is known as *proportionate stratification*.

stratifying factor

proportionate stratification

SAQ 10

Using the data in the table in Appendix 1, stratify the institutions proportionately by country and distribute a sample of 10 between them as in Table 3. Comment briefly on your results and suggest a solution to those problems you identify.

Disproportionate Stratification

5.5 So far we have assumed that *all* members of the sample population have had a uniform probability of selection. But in many real-life situations this approach will not always yield the most 'efficient' design. By less *efficient*, we mean that for the same cost it would be less precise (in the sense of having a larger standard error) than could be achieved using some alternative design.

5.6 It may also be the case, for instance, that we wish to analyse the results from some strata separately, and proportionate stratification may result in the size of sample from one or more of these strata being too small for the precision we want. Conversely, with disproportionate stratification, the size of sample from a stratum may be larger than we need to achieve a given level of precision. Let us look briefly at another example.

5.7 *Example 3* Suppose we wanted a sample of 1600 finally registered students on OU Arts Faculty courses in 1976, stratified by level of the course, in order to estimate (among other things) the proportion who listen to more than half of the radio programmes. See Table 4, but ignore for the moment, the fact that some students will be studying at more than one level.

Table 4

	Population size	%	Sample size (propor-tionate)	Sample size (dispropor-tionate)	f
Column no.	(i)	(ii)	(iii)	(iv)	(v)
Foundation	5 209	31	496	400	- ⵍ77
First level	6 938	41	656	400	. ⵍ58
Second level	4 512	26	416	400	. 089
Third level	400	2	32	400	1
Total	17 059	100	1 600	1 600	

5.8 In column (ii) we have calculated the percentage distribution of the population between the strata. These percentages are then applied to the sample size of 1600, the resultant sample size in each stratum being shown in column (iii). As you can see, the sample sizes in the different strata vary from 656 to 32. Suppose we decide that a minimum sample of 400 in each stratum is needed. If, in our example, we wanted to analyse the results from each of the strata separately, and assuming we did not need to analyse separately any sub-groups within any of the strata, then our sample would be most efficient if the sample size was approximately 400 in each stratum.

5.9 To achieve these figures, however, we would have to distribute the sample between the strata in proportions which differed from the population distribution. This is called *disproportionate stratification*. In our example, we have decided to distribute the sample equally between all four strata. The main advantage of doing this, apart from possibly making the sample more efficient, is that equal sized samples are needed for some types of multi-variate analyses, e.g. with two-way analysis of variance (which you will meet in Block 7). If this sort of analysis is not

disproportionate stratification

to be used, then some other breakdown of the sample into disproportionate-sized strata could be used to improve precision and efficiency.

SAQ 11
In Example 3 (paragraphs 5.7 and 5.8), assume you wish to distribute the sample equally between all four strata. Complete Table 4 by calculating f for each stratum and enter your results into column (v).

5.10 *Summary* By using a stratified sample design it is possible to *control* the representation in the sample of the parts of the population in the different strata, in relation to the stratifying factor. We can do this either by ensuring that the sample contains the same proportion in each stratum that we would find in the population (proportionate stratification) or by deliberately changing the proportions in each stratum (disproportionate stratification).

Effects on the Standard Error

5.11 As we have seen, stratification increases the precision of the sample results for a given sample size by *ensuring* that either the sample cannot differ from the population with respect to the stratifying factor (proportionate stratification) or that the researcher controls any such differences (as in the case of disproportionate stratification). This means that the standard errors are smaller than you would get with a random sample of the same size. In other words, the distribution of all possible samples of that size is not as spread out for a stratified sample as for a random sample because the researcher, through stratification, has ensured that the part of the variability of the population due to the existence of the different groups is represented in the sample in a way which is predetermined by himself or herself (see Figures 5 and 6).

Figure 5   Simple random sample: distribution of all possible samples of size *n*

Figure 6   Stratified sample: distribution of all possible samples of size *n*

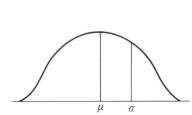

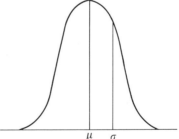

5.12 The *total error variance* (i.e. the standard error squared) of a variable or proportion in a stratified sample is simply the weighted sum of all the *stratum error variances*. Now, with a stratified sample, we have in effect several random samples, one in each stratum, each with its own variance. The more *homogeneous* the population within a stratum is with respect to the characteristic we are investigating, and therefore the less the variance, the less the standard error will be (see Figure 7), and of course the less the contribution of each stratum is to the total error variance, the greater will be the *reduction* in the total error variance. At worst, if the population in each stratum is completely *heterogeneous* with respect to some characteristic, then the variance for that variable will be the same as that for a simple random sample of the same size. However, as Moser and Kalton (1971, p. 95) point out, with disproportionate stratification the sampling fractions that are best for *one* of the variables being studied may not be

total error variance, stratum error variance

homogeneity

heterogeneity

the best for another. In other words, while a reduction in the standard error for one particular variable may be obtained by varying the proportions of the sample taken from the different strata in a particular way, this may well be at the expense of *increasing* the standard error for another variable. In general, therefore, proportionate stratification of the sample will normally result in a smaller standard error than would be obtained with the same size random sample (i.e. greater precision is achieved) and, at worst will never have less precision than with a simple random sample of the same size; this is not the case with disproportionate stratification where reductions in the error for one variable may well be at the expense of increases in error for another variable.

Figure 7   Effect of homogeneity of population with respect to characteristic *X*, on the distribution of all possible samples

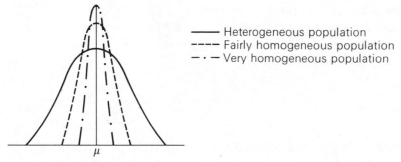

5.13   Other major reasons for using stratification are:

(a)   Where separate estimates from different groups within the population are wanted for comparison purposes. In such instances, the desired representation can be *ensured* by selecting separate samples from each group.

(b)   For administrative convenience; for example, when different parts of the frame are in different places (as with Local Authority rating lists) rather than being held together in one place.

(c)   Where different sampling procedures need to be used for different parts of the population; for example, in the Sample Census of 1966, hotels and institutions were sampled differently from private households.

5.14   The only major problem associated with any method of stratification is that the variables available for stratification purposes are limited to those in the frames and these may not group the population into particularly homogeneous strata. Hence, only relatively small gains in precision are achieved. On the other hand, with proportionate allocation, these gains can often be achieved for very little effort, particularly if the frame is already stratified (for example, separate personnel records for each establishment in a large firm).

5.15   *Summary*   Because of its convenience, and because the precision is, in practice, never less than for a simple random sample of the same size, proportionate stratification is generally the most popular method in practice.

6   Cluster Sampling

6.1   Whenever a small sample is wanted from a large population which is spread over a wide area, there are added to the costs of the study two major expenses. These are listing the population to compile the sampling frame and interviewers'/ field workers' travel. For example, the construction of a complete frame of mothers with young children who live in a certain county, or of small firms, or of high-yield cows would be extremely time-consuming and expensive. Even if the right sort of frame was available, the costs of travelling round to a scattered sample would be prohibitive. In effect, the problem is how to reconcile the trade-off between statistical precision and cost.

6.2   We can avoid many of these practical difficulties by the use of *cluster sampling*. Clusters are naturally occurring or purposely grouped sets of elements. Hence, *cluster sampling involves the selection (either randomly or systematically) of whole groups*, that is clusters, which by definition must contain more than one element of the population.

cluster sampling

6.3   It is, of course, essential that each element belongs to only one cluster. Examples of clusters are:

(a)   Classes in schools, where children are the elements.

(b)   Cartons of packaged goods, where the goods are the elements.

(c)   Herds of cows, where the cows are the elements.

(d)   Branches of firms, where the employees (say) are the elements.

(e)   Geographical areas, where almost anything could be elements.

Single-stage Cluster Sampling

6.4   The price which has to be paid, however, for reducing costs is the (probable) reduction of precision. We saw earlier that with stratification homogeneity within strata was necessary. Let us now consider two extreme situations for clustering. Suppose each cluster was completely homogeneous. If we selected 10 clusters, each containing around 100 elements, we would in effect have a sample of only 10 different items. On the other hand, if the elements in each cluster were completely heterogeneous, we would in effect have a sample of $10 \times 100 = 1000$. *At best*, therefore a cluster sample will have the same standard error as a simple random sample of the same total size, while *at worst* it will have the same standard error as a simple random sample whose size equals the number of clusters in the cluster sample. In practice, of course, the level of error is somewhere between these two extremes. Thus, unlike stratification, if clusters are being purposively formed, the elements a cluster contains should be as *heterogeneous* as possible, with the effect that each cluster will be similar to other clusters so that as little information as possible is lost due to those clusters in the population that are not included in the sample.

6.5   In general, cluster sampling is introduced into situations where:

(a)   the saving in costs compensates or more than compensates for the increase in standard error and increased costs of analysis; or

(b)   there is no alternative: that is, where the elements can only be identified after a cluster has been selected. For example, suppose we want to select a sample of workers. Whereas we can reasonably compile a frame of employers, it is extremely difficult, if not impossible, to compile a frame of workers as such. The employers are willing to contact their workers on our behalf, but will not usually give us access to their personnel records. In this sort of situation the only method of sampling open to us is to cluster sample. We can only select a sample of employers (clusters of workers).

The effect of using clusters may be seen more clearly if we look at another example.

6.6   *Example 4*   Suppose that a town has 9000 school-age children in 360 different classes with a mean size of 25 pupils per class and we wish to select a sample of 200 pupils. We could select a simple random sample of 200 pupils. On the other hand if we decide to use cluster sampling, using the classes as clusters, then roughly the same sample size would arise from 8 classes. As a certain amount of homogeneity would be expected within each selected class (for example, same age, living in the same area, same ability group), a less precise picture of the population would accrue from the cluster sample than from the simple random sample, in that 25 children, say, from the same class would give a more limited picture of the population than 25 children from up to 25 different classes. In addition we would not be certain of selecting exactly 200 children as the size of the sample would be determined by the size of the clusters selected.

Multi-stage Cluster Sampling

6.7   Suppose that there was no alternative to using a cluster sample. After the initial clusters (usually called *primary sampling units* or *psu*'s) were selected, another stage of selection could be introduced by selecting a sample of elements from *within* the selected clusters. This would be a two-stage sample. This process can be taken even further. After the initial clusters, or primary sampling units, have been selected, it is often possible to sub-divide each one into further clusters; these would be called *secondary sampling units*. A sample of these secondary units could then be taken from each selected primary sampling unit. Again, clusters could be formed within the secondary sampling units and a further selection could take place, and so on for as many stages as required. This process is called *multi-stage cluster sampling*.

primary sampling unit (psu)

secondary sampling unit

multi-stage cluster sampling

6.8   *Example 5*   Suppose that we want to select a national sample of school children. In a multi-stage cluster sample, we might proceed as follows:

First stage   – selection of a sample of Local Education Authorities

Second stage – selection of a sample of schools within each selected LEA

Third stage   – selection of a sample of children within each selected school

6.9   When would you use a multi-stage design? Basically there are three types of situation when you would expect a multi-stage design to be used:

(a)   If the sampling frame was inadequate, the initial frame need only contain details of the first stage of clusters or primary sampling units (*psus*). At each successive stage new details could be collected from each of the selected units to enable the next stage of selection to take place, as in Example 5.

(b)   Multi-stage selection can compensate to a certain extent for the effects of clustering by in effect 'spreading' the sample.

(c)   In situations where you wish to control the size of the sample selected from each primary sampling unit (psu). The most common way of doing this is by selecting primary sampling units with *probability proportionate to size (pps)*, as was done in the Plowden survey. This entails accumulating the sizes of successive clusters and then drawing the sample from a list of those totals. An example is shown in Table 5: the cumulative totals are shown in column (ii) and the selected samples in column (iii). What this technique does is ensure that the chance of selecting any psu (in this case, University) varies in proportion to its size – hence the name of this particular technique. At the second stage of selection, equal sized samples are then selected from each of the selected psus.

probability proportionate to size (pps)

Notes to Table 5 (right):

A random start, 8091, has been selected in the sampling interval 00001–21762. This identifies the first university. The other nine are obtained for the sample by adding the sampling interval 21762·5 to this number successively.

London University has been selected twice (a function of size). In a case like this two equal-sized samples would be selected from within the selected primary unit.

Source: Statistics of Education – Universities, Vol 6, 1968, 1970, p. 48

Table 5   Sample of 10 universities selected with probability proportional to size

		All students (including those on courses not of a university standard) (i)			Cumulative totals (ii)	Sample of 10 selected with pps (iii)
		Men	Women	Total		
1	Aston	2,436	267	2,703	2 703	
2	Bath....................................	1,566	293	1,859	4 562	
3	Birmingham	4,705	2,054	6,759	11 321	← 8 091
4	Bradford	2,708	441	3,149	14 470	
5	Bristol	3,907	2,058	5,965	20 435	
6	Brunel	1,247	194	1,441	21 876	
7	Cambridge	9,208	1,208	10,416	32 292	← 29 853·5
8	City	2,161	158	2,319	34 611	
9	Durham	2,222	1,011	3,233	37 844	
10	East Anglia	1,306	820	2,126	39 970	
11	Essex	1,007	471	1,478	41 448	
12	Exeter	1,916	1,140	3,056	44 504	
13	Hull	2,425	1,266	3,691	48 195	
14	Keele	1,096	719	1,815	50 010	
15	Kent	1,146	736	1,882	51 892	← 51 616
16	Lancaster	1,296	607	1,903	53 795	
17	Leeds	6,012	2,459	8,471	62 266	
18	Leicester..............................	1,831	1,290	3,121	65 387	
19	Liverpool	4,634	1,757	6,391	71 778	
20	London Graduate School of Business Studies	98	2	100	71 878	←⎰78 378·5
21	London University	22,494	9,039	31,533	103 411	⎱95 141
22	Loughborough	2,030	149	2,179	105 590	
23	Manchester Business School	52	3	55	105 645	
24	Manchester University.................	5,224	2,622	7,846	113 491	
25	University of Manchester Institute of Science and Technology	2,818	249	3,067	116 558	
26	Newcastle	3,843	1,568	5,411	121 969	← 116 903·5
27	Nottingham	3,409	1,594	5,003	126 972	
28	Oxford	8,505	1,977	10,482	137 454	
29	Reading	2,887	1,727	4,614	142 068	←138 666
30	Salford	2,968	254	3,222	145 290	
31	Sheffield	4,028	1,528	5,556	150 246	
32	Southampton	2,998	1,133	4,131	154 977	
33	Surrey	1,768	463	2,231	157 208	
34	Sussex	2,352	1,105	3,457	160 665	←160 428
35	Warwick	1,019	527	1,546	162 211	
36	York	1,114	807	1,921	164 132	
37	**Total England**	120,436	43,696	164,132		
38	Aberystwyth University College ...	1,430	890	2,320	166 452	
39	Bangor University College	1,596	831	2,427	168 879	
40	Cardiff University College	1,980	1,155	3,135	172 014	
41	St. David's, Lampeter	208	78	286	172 300	
42	Swansea University College	2,241	1,133	3,374	175 674	
43	Welsh National School of Medicine	251	81	332	176 006	
44	University of Wales Insitute of Science and Technology	1,484	178	1,662	177 668	
45	**Total Wales**	9,190	4,346	13,536		
46	**Total England and Wales**	129,626	48,042	177,668		
47	Aberdeen	3,205	1,804	5,009	182 677	←182 191
48	Dundee	1,825	580	2,405	185 082	
49	Edinburgh	5,830	3,363	9,193	194 275	
50	Glasgow	5,315	2,383	7,698	201 973	
51	Heriot-Watt	1,662	187	1,849	203 822	
52	St. Andrews	1,343	962	2,305	206 127	←203 953·5
53	Stirling	186	144	330	206 457	
54	Strathclyde.............................	3,921	1,107	5,028	211 425	
55	**Total Scotland**	23,287	10,530	33,817		
56	**Total Great Britain**	152,913	58,572	211,485		
57	Queen's University, Belfast	4,089	1,659	5,748	217 233	
58	University of Ulster, Coleraine	208	184	392	217 625	
59	**Total Northern Ireland**	4,297	1,843	6,140		
60	**Total United Kingdom**	157,210	60,415	217,625		

$$f = \frac{217\ 625}{10} = \frac{1}{21\ 762 \cdot 5}$$

31

7 Calculation and Presentation of Standard Errors

7.1   We have now covered the main types of sample design and looked at their effect on the precision of samples. But there can be a major problem when it comes to deciding how detailed the information about the precision of individual statistics or measures should be in the final research report and, conversely, what sort of detail you would expect to find in a research report.

7.2   The problem arises basically because of the number of statistics involved. Every statistic on each table is an estimate, whether it be an aggregate, mean, or proportion, and even in the most modest pieces of research there can be scores of tables. The cost of computing the standard errors for all these thousands of statistics (one 10×10 table alone gives 100 statistics) could eat up most of the analysis budget.

7.3   Even if the cash were available, would it be desirable to present the reader with multiple sets of tables? At a minimum there would be one table of standard errors for each table of research findings and if comparisons between pairs of statistics were to be made, the situation would be worse still. Not surprisingly, most readers would find this very confusing; it is not necessary for the majority and it could even be counter-productive in that important findings could sink without trace in the sea of tables. That is not to say that the researcher should go to the other extreme and give no indication of the level of error associated with the research findings, although it must be admitted that this is not an uncommon occurrence.

7.4   It should be stated straightaway that there are no easy solutions to this problem, no commonly agreed 'correct' strategy. All I can do in this Part is to outline some of the more common approaches.

(a)   Reader calculates own standard errors. This is possible when an srs design has been used or where the effect of the design is sufficiently close to an srs design. A term you might come across in this connection is *design effect (Deff)*. The design effect is simply the ratio of the actual error variance of the sample statistic to the error variance of an srs sample of the same size. Thus a stratified sample would have a Deff of less than 1, whereas a cluster sample would usually have a Deff greater than 1. Where Deff $= 1$, then you are using a design which has achieved the same level of error as that associated with an srs design (this is often the aim of a stratified cluster design).

design effect (Deff)

(b)   The standard errors for major findings can be calculated, and presented alongside the findings.

(c)   A *range* of standard errors can be calculated so that the reader knows the best and worst situation. In practice, this probably means the standard error is overestimated.

(d)   The design effect (Deff) for groups of statistics can be calculated. There can be considerable theoretical problems associated with this approach and it is, therefore, not normally used in smaller studies.

8 Concluding Remarks

8.1   Sample design is both a science and an art. Given the same problem, two researchers could come up with two different designs, both of them 'correct' insofar as their own research priorities are concerned. This is not to say, however, that no incorrect or bad decisions are ever made.

8.2 Having studied this section on sampling, you should now be in a position to assess both the statistical validity of a sample design as reported in a research report, and the efficiency of the design used. To help you do this, a check-list of decision points in the development of a sample design is included in Appendix B.

Objectives

After reading this Part you should be able to:

1 Distinguish between a census, non-probability and probability sample and state the main advantages and disadvantages of each of them (paragraphs 2.13–2.16, 3.1–3.18).

2 Describe the steps involved in drawing up an efficient sampling frame (paragraphs 3.19 and 3.20).

3 State the procedures for drawing a simple random sample from a population using a table of random numbers (paragraphs 4.4 to 4.6).

4 Calculate the standard error of a mean and a proportion for a simple random sample and explain their use in setting confidence intervals for population estimates (paragraphs 4.19–4.30).

5 Distinguish between a simple random sample, systematic sample, stratified sample and multi-stage cluster sample (paragraphs 4.1–4.3, 4.7–4.10, 5.1–5.10, 6.7–6.9).

6 Define the terms precision and efficiency in relation to sample design and explain the relationship between precision, efficiency and cost (paragraphs 2.14–2.16, 3.10–3.11, 4.27–4.30).

Appendix A: Sampling Frames: Universities in the United Kingdom, 1968

Number of full-time students at 31 December 1968

		All students (including those on courses not of a university standard)			Undergraduate level					
					All students		From outside the United Kingdom		Entering for the first time in 1968–69	
		Men	Women	Total	Men	Women	Men	Women	Men	Women
1	Aston	2,436	267	2,703	2,110	234	70	2	695	95
2	Bath	1,566	293	1,859	1,377	236	42	9	467	80
3	Birmingham	4,705	2,054	6,759	3,429	1,703	127	20	1,066	564
4	Bradford	2,708	441	3,149	2,306	418	55	7	694	161
5	Bristol	3,907	2,058	5,965	3,177	1,799	81	34	1,096	702
6	Brunel	1,247	194	1,441	1,165	171	13	4	360	65
7	Cambridge	9,208	1,208	10,416	7,371	900	244	43	2,455	331
8	City	2,161	158	2,319	1,972	140	51	6	542	48
9	Durham	2,222	1,011	3,233	1,742	885	22	24	654	353
10	East Anglia	1,306	820	2,126	1,124	793	17	20	437	285
11	Essex	1,007	471	1,478	773	419	18	9	334	163
12	Exeter	1,916	1,140	3,056	1,599	1,010	74	48	592	377
13	Hull	2,425	1,266	3,691	2,098	1,150	66	17	769	437
14	Keele	1,096	719	1,815	954	673	8	8	262	166
15	Kent	1,146	736	1,882	1,001	709	15	8	383	249
16	Lancaster	1,296	607	1,903	1,054	577	32	10	529	292
17	Leeds	6,012	2,459	8,471	4,933	2,161	270	56	1,763	841
18	Leicester	1,831	1,290	3,121	1,482	1,091	55	19	585	413
19	Liverpool	4,634	1,757	6,391	3,739	1,478	95	4	1,135	462
20	London Graduate School of Business Studies	98	2	100	—	—	—	—	—	—
21	London University	22,494	9,039	31,533	15,988	6,757	1,003	353	5,325	2,421
22	Loughborough	2,030	149	2,179	1,744	124	111	2	522	67
23	Manchester Business School	52	3	55	—	—	—	—	—	—
24	Manchester University	5,224	2,622	7,846	4,206	2,252	201	63	1,372	778
25	University of Manchester Institute of Science and Technology	2,818	249	3,067	2,081	219	171	8	766	91
26	Newcastle	3,843	1,568	5,411	3,241	1,402	243	40	1,065	467
27	Nottingham	3,409	1,594	5,003	2,607	1,321	58	25	979	483
28	Oxford	8,505	1,977	10,482	6,218	1,425	329	31	2,051	485
29	Reading	2,887	1,727	4,614	2,417	1,577	116	53	972	631
30	Salford	2,968	254	3,222	2,610	238	67	3	920	96
31	Sheffield	4,028	1,528	5,556	3,292	1,342	122	17	1,121	449
32	Southampton	2,998	1,133	4,131	2,313	959	78	16	831	309
33	Surrey	1,768	463	2,231	1,451	441	97	10	503	192
34	Sussex	2,352	1,105	3,457	1,757	956	54	39	626	306
35	Warwick	1,019	527	1,546	810	503	16	9	317	216
36	York	1,114	807	1,921	894	694	30	21	337	282
37	**Total England**	120,436	43,696	164,132	95,035	36,757	4,051	1,038	32,525	13,357
38	Aberystwyth University College	1,430	890	2,320	1,166	753	10	3	418	251
39	Bangor University College	1,596	831	2,427	1,216	709	38	7	427	232
40	Cardiff University College	1,980	1,155	3,135	1,673	985	94	15	672	347
41	St. David's, Lampeter	208	78	286	177	78	—	—	53	19
42	Swansea University College	2,241	1,133	3,374	1,843	989	92	24	612	325
43	Welsh National School of Medicine	251	81	332	247	57	7	—	94	15
44	University of Wales Insitute of Science and Technology	1,484	178	1,662	1,374	159	54	2	470	54
45	**Total Wales**	9,190	4,346	13,536	7,696	3,730	295	51	2,746	1,243
46	**Total England and Wales**	129,626	48,042	177,668	102,731	40,487	4,346	1,089	35,271	14,600
47	Aberdeen	3,205	1,804	5,009	2,915	1,696	65	16	883	555
48	Dundee	1,825	580	2,405	1,626	521	40	8	458	150
49	Edinburgh	5,830	3,363	9,193	4,871	3,055	193	104	1,283	973
50	Glasgow	5,315	2,383	7,698	4,803	2,219	158	17	1,353	710
51	Heriot-Watt	1,662	187	1,849	1,578	184	184	6	703	62
52	St. Andrews	1,343	962	2,305	1,188	934	54	33	495	304
53	Stirling	186	144	330	148	139	—	—	81	64
54	Strathclyde	3,921	1,107	5,028	3,429	986	197	7	1,145	288
55	**Total Scotland**	23,287	10,530	33,817	20,558	9,734	891	191	6,401	3,106
56	**Total Great Britain**	152,913	58,572	211,485	123,289	50,221	5,237	1,280	41,672	17,706
57	Queen's University, Belfast	4,089	1,659	5,748	3,627	1,529	96	25	1,047	494
58	University of Ulster, Coleraine	208	184	392	159	123	4	6	159	123
59	**Total Northern Ireland**	4,297	1,843	6,140	3,786	1,652	100	31	1,206	617
60	**Total United Kingdom**	157,210	60,415	217,625	127,075	51,873	5,337	1,311	42,878	18,323

Source: Statistics of Education – Universities, Vol. 6, 1968, 1970, p. 48

Appendix B: Decision Points in the Development of a Sample Design

The decision about which sampling method to use will always depend on the particular problems that are identified at the time of sampling. Similarly, the cost of using a particular method will always play a dominant role in determining which method is feasible. Nevertheless, decisions about the sample design must always be taken after certain questions have been asked.

1 (a) Is a sampling frame available and accessible?
  (b) What deficiencies, if any, does the frame have?

2 (a) Is stratification to be used?
  (b) What variables should be used for stratification?
  (c) What form of stratification should be used:
    (i) proportionate?
    (ii) disproportionate?

3 (a) Is cluster sampling necessary?
  (b) How many stages will be needed?
  (c) Will the primary sampling units be selected using
    (i) probability proportionate to size?
    (ii) uniform probability?

4 How will the actual population elements be selected:
    (a) by simple random sample with or without replacement?
    (b) systematically?

It is perhaps as well to remember that although one needs some form of mental checklist such as the one above, the best sample designs are the simplest.

I don't think *he* would mind if we assumed there was only one eagle-owl in that nest

Answers to Self-assessment Questions

SAQ 1

To arrive at the working population you should:

(a) Outline the theoretical basis for selecting your population.

(b) Define the population explicitly and unambiguously.

(c) Check that it can be identified.

(d) Check that it is accessible.

Redefine, if necessary, in the light of the problems which have arisen.

SAQ 2

If we looked at the distribution of all the grades that all the students have got over the year on DE304 we would be carrying out a *census* of the students on that course, but a *sample survey* of the students on (say) all 'D' courses or all Third Level courses. The sample would *not* be a representative one. It could, however, be termed a *case study* (see paragraph 3.8 on non-probability sampling). If we had widened the scope of the study and examined the grades of all Third Level 'D' courses, this could be either a census of Third Level 'D' courses or a sample (albeit a non-representative one) of all Third Level courses or all 'D' courses etc.

SAQ 3

In order to define the population, you should first identify the main variables by which you want to limit the population. This stage will depend to a large extent on your research purpose (and theoretical bases) for selecting the population (you are interested in), but also in part on your knowledge of the structure of the population. You might, for instance, want to restrict your population by such variables as:

(a) Employment status, e.g. employed full-time, or employed more than 3 full days per week, etc.

(b) Type of educational establishment, e.g. first schools in maintained sector only.

(c) Qualifications, e.g. recognized as qualified by the DES (thus excluding such categories as student teachers).

(d) Geographical area, e.g. Scotland only, or a specified LEA.

(e) Status, e.g. exclude Head teachers with no time-tabled class.

(f) Point in time, e.g. contact on a certain date. (This would then include temporary teachers.)

The variables you do not use as limiting factors would then automatically be included, e.g. both sexes, graduates and non-graduates, etc.

Identification should not prove a problem as employed teachers could be identified through the schools they were working in on a certain date.

Finally, teachers may have moved on to other schools, and you then have the problem of tracking them down.
rather than letting you approach the teachers directly at school, they might prefer to ask the teachers themselves whether or not they wish to participate. At the worst, of course, they might flatly refuse to give you access to the teachers. Finally, teachers may have moved on to other schools, and you then have the problem of tracking them down.

Redefining the population: if access to any specific group proves a real problem (e.g. with temporary teachers) you may decide to redefine your population by excluding this group. Similarly, if, after identification, it looks too costly to include teachers in certain schools (e.g. small schools with only two or three teachers) then you may decide to exclude this group if you consider the additional cost of including them is more important than the worth of the data you would gain.

SAQ 4

A combination of the two would be most appropriate if the time allowed. Because the researchers know very little about the area they wish to investigate, they cannot adequately describe their working population (i.e. students involved in informal study networks) at this stage.

Their first job must, therefore, be to learn sufficient about student networks to enable them to define and categorize them. To do this, they could possibly use a variation of snowball sampling by contacting students who were known to be participating in such networks by regional counselling and tutorial staff. Once the researchers could adequately define and describe the type of student activity they were interested in, they could follow this stage by a second stage, which would be a probability sample which would enable them to produce estimates. (You may remember that this is the sequence recommended for carrying out any survey – see paragraph 3.4.)

SAQ 5

It depends on what the researcher states or assumes her working population is. If the working population is students who attended on that night, then it is a probability sample. If, however, the working population is assumed to be wider, say students who normally attend on that evening of the week (some of whom might not have attended on that day) or students who have ever attended study centres, or all students, then it is not a probability sample because some of the working population would have been excluded from selection (i.e. those who had not attended a study centre on the night in question).

SAQ 6

The institutions are already numbered so you can use those numbers. You will notice that numbers have also been assigned to sub-totals, e.g. 37 is 'Total England'. Do not worry about this as if you select these numbers you can treat them as ineligibles.

Now in the table in Appendix 1, $N = 60$, so you choose 2 digits. Starting from line 07, you have:
98 x (treated as a blank since 98 > 60)
85 x (treated as a blank since 85 > 60)
17 Leeds
81 x (treated as a blank since 81 > 60)
63 x (treated as a blank since 63 > 60)
61 x (treated as a blank since 61 > 60)
42 Swansea University College
45 x (treated as a blank because it is not a number assigned to an institution)
40 Cardiff University College
54 Strathclyde
49 Edinburgh
80 x (treated as a blank since 80 > 60)
07 Cambridge
(restart at line 07)
74 x (treated as a blank since 74 > 60)
02 Bath
77 x (treated as a blank since 77 > 60)
83 x (treated as a blank since 83 > 60)
78 x (treated as a blank since 78 > 60)
84 x (treated as a blank since 84 > 60)
24 Manchester University
23 Manchester Business School
33 Surrey

SAQ 7

Recalling the discussion on sampling frames (paragraphs 3.18–3.20), we should either adjust the sample size to allow for the ineligibles, or sort them out before sampling. Because our population is so small, it is easiest to sort out the ineligibles first.

Now, $N = 53$

$\qquad n = 10$

$\therefore \qquad f = \dfrac{10}{53} = \dfrac{1}{5.3}$

RS $= 4$ Bradford

  4   $+ 5.3 =$ 9.3   (10) East Anglia

  9.3 $+ 5.3 = 14.6$ (15) Kent

14.6 $+ 5.3 = 19.9$ (20) London Graduate School of Business Studies

19.9 $+ 5.3 = 25.2$ (26) Newcastle

25.2 $+ 5.3 = 30.5$ (31) Sheffield

30.5 $+ 5.3 = 35.8$ (36) York

35.8 $+ 5.3 = 41.1$ (42) Welsh National School of Medicine

41.1 $+ 5.3 = 46.4$ (47) Glasgow

46.4 $+ 5.3 = 51.7$ (52) Queen's University, Belfast

51.7 $+ 5.3 = 57.0 \, x$

The frame is ordered by country and, within country, alphabetically by institution.

The sample you selected using random selection had 6 institutions from England (out of 36), 2 from Wales (out of 7) and 2 from Scotland (out of 8). There were none selected from Northern Ireland. It could be argued that English Universities were underrepresented here. How serious this is would depend on the subject of the research and whether it was related in any way to regions or geographical areas. If it was, the fact that two of the six selected English institutions are in the same city, Manchester, would exacerbate the problem. With systematic selection because of the way the frame is ordered, you are bound to get the sample distributed between the different countries in the right proportions, and of course it would be impossible to select more than one institution from the same town or city.

SAQ 8

The sample estimate of the mean size of UK institutions is:

$$\bar{X} = \frac{\Sigma X}{n} = \frac{35\,418}{10} = 3541.8$$

Now for the standard error of the estimate, we use:

$$s_{\bar{x}} = \sqrt{(1-f)}\,\frac{s}{\sqrt{n}} \quad \text{(paragraph 4.20, see also paragraph 4.19)}$$

where,

$$s = \sqrt{\frac{\Sigma(X_i - \bar{X})^2}{n-1}}$$

X_i	$\bar{X}$	$X_i - \bar{X}$	$(X_i - \bar{X})^2$
3149	3542	$-$ 393	154 449
2126		-1416	2 005 056
1882		-1660	2 755 600
100		-3442	11 847 364
5411		1869	3 493 161
5556		2014	4 056 196
1921		-1621	2 627 641
332		-3210	10 304 100
9193		5651	31 933 801
5748		2206	4 866 436

$\Sigma(X_i - \bar{X})^2 = 74\,043\,804$

$$s = \sqrt{\frac{\Sigma(X_i - \bar{X})^2}{n-1}} = \sqrt{\frac{74\,043\,804}{9}}$$

$$ = \sqrt{8\,227\,089.3}$$

$$ = 2868.3$$

Now,

$$\sqrt{(1-f)} = \sqrt{1 - \frac{1}{5.3}} = \sqrt{0.8113}$$
$$= 0.9$$
$$\sqrt{n} = \sqrt{10}$$
$$= 3.16$$

Therefore,

$$s_{\bar{x}} = \sqrt{(1-f)} \, \frac{s}{\sqrt{n}} = 0.9 \times \frac{2868.3}{3.16}$$
$$= 0.9 \times 907.7$$
$$= 816.9$$

SAQ 9

The worst possible case would occur when $p = q = 0.5$ (i.e. 50%).
From the formula in paragraph 4.21, we know that

$$s_p = (1-f) \sqrt{\frac{pq}{n}}$$

We can ignore the factor $(1-f)$ as f is less than $\frac{1}{10}$, $\left(\text{i.e. } f = \frac{40}{10\,000} = \frac{1}{250}\right)$

Substituting in for the remainder of the formula, we get:

$$s_p = \sqrt{\left(\frac{0.5 \times 0.5}{40}\right)} = \sqrt{\left(\frac{0.25}{40}\right)}$$

To transform into a percentage, multiply by 100 giving:

$$s_p = \sqrt{\left(\frac{0.25}{40}\right) \times 100^2} \, \% = \sqrt{\frac{2500}{40}} \, \%$$
$$= \sqrt{(62.5)}\%$$
$$= 7.9\%$$

Note   At the 95% level of confidence, we would be talking about a sample proportion of 50% ± 2(7.9)%, or 50% ± 15.8%, in other words a confidence interval of 34.2% to 65.8%. Although this is a rather wide range it could be quite adequate for some purposes. Take for instance research on usage of facilities: an organization may only need to know that at least $x\%$ of the working population will use a facility; if overcrowding is likely to be a problem that not more than $y\%$ are likely to use it at any one time.

SAQ 10

Stratum	Population size	Percentage of total in each stratum	Sample size	Rounded sample size
England	36	68	6·8	7
Wales	7	13	1·3	1
Scotland	8	15	1·5	2
N. Ireland	2	4	0·4	0
Total	53	100	10	10

The main problem arises because of the variation between the sizes of the strata and because of the small size of the strata. One stratum, Northern Ireland, ends up with no sample at all, while another stratum, Wales, ends up with a sample of 1. In fact (think about this) a sample of 1 is statistically useless as there is no way of measuring the standard deviation (and hence standard error) with only one measurement. If it is important that each of the strata are represented in the sample, then you would have to assign a minimum sample of 2 to each of the smallest strata. Thus, to retain proportionate stratification you would need a larger total sample, or, if this was not possible, you would have to retain what is in effect, a *disproportionate* stratified sample (see paragraphs 5.5 to 5.10).

SAQ 11

	Population size	%	Sample size (proportionate)	Sample size (dis-proportionate)	*f*
Column no.	(i)	(ii)	(iii)	(iv)	(v)
Foundation	5 209	31	496	400	1/13
First level	6 938	41	656	400	1/17
Second level	4 512	26	416	400	1/11
Third level	400	2	32	400	All=1/1
Total	17 059	100	1 600	1 600	

References

BYNNER, J. and STRIBLEY, K. M. (eds) (1979) *Social research: principles and procedures*, London, Longman/The Open University Press (Course Reader).

HEDGES, B. (1979) 'Sampling minority populations', in Wilson, M. J. (ed.) (1979) Ch. 12.

KISH, L. (1965) *Survey sampling*, New York, John Wiley and Sons.

MILGRAM, S. (1963) 'Behavioral study of obedience', *Journal of Abnormal and Social Psychology*, Vol. 67, pp. 371–8. Reprinted in Wilson, M. J. (ed.) (1979) Ch. 10.

MOSER, C. A. and KALTON, G. (1971) *Survey methods in social investigations*, London, Heinemann.

PLOWDEN REPORT (1967) *Children and their primary schools*, Central Advisory Council for Education (England), Vol. 1: Report, Vol. 2: Research and Surveys, London, HMSO.

SMITH, H. W. (1975) *Strategies of social research: the methodological imagination*, Englewood Cliffs, N. J., Prentice-Hall (Set Book).

WILMOTT, P. and YOUNG, M. D. (1960) *Family and class in a London suburb*, London, Routledge and Kegan Paul.

WILSON, M. J. (ed.) (1979) *Social and educational research in action: a book of readings*, London, Longman/The Open University Press (Course Reader).

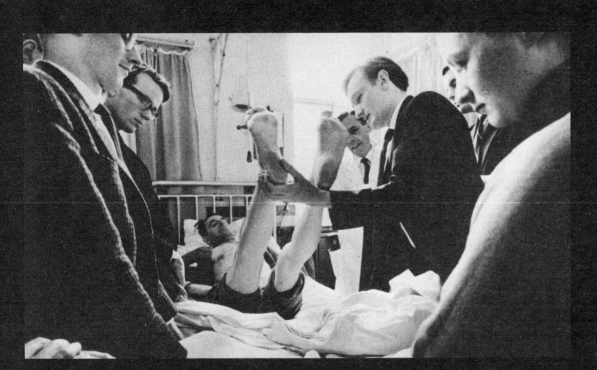

Part 5 Research Design in Ethnography
Prepared by Paul Atkinson for the Course Team

Block 3 Part 5

Contents

Aim

To introduce the planning and design of ethnographic research, from the manner in which research questions are posed to the general considerations involved in gaining access, entering, sampling and participating in the research setting.

Study Guide

I have indicated in the correspondence text the most appropriate points for you to read the set and recommended readings. There are a number of activities in the text which I hope you will find useful. In the case of ITQs the answers follow immediately in the correspondence text, while those for the SAQs are at the end of this Part. The latter are not necessarily the only answers but are my own notes, intended to act as a guide as to the kind of answer required where you are invited to use your own examples, as in SAQ 2 and SAQ 8.

Set Reading

LACEY, C. (1976) 'Problems of sociological fieldwork: a review of the methodology of *Hightown Grammar*', in Wilson, M. J. (ed.) (1979) *Social and educational research in action: a book of readings*, Ch. 8.

WHYTE, W. F. (1955) 'Methodological appendix', in *Street corner society*, sections 4, 5 and 6 only. (Edited version is supplied as Supplementary Material.)

Recommended Reading

BECKER, H. S. and GEER, B. (1958) 'The fate of idealism in medical school', in Wilson, M. J. (ed.) (1979) *Social and educational research in action: a book of readings*, Ch. 15.

WHYTE, W. F. (1955) 'Methodological appendix', in *Street corner society*. (Edited version supplied as Supplementary Material.)

WISEMAN, J. P. (1974) 'The research web', in Bynner, J. and Stribley, K. M. (eds) (1979) *Social research: principles and procedures*, Ch. 10.

A: ETHNOGRAPHIC RESEARCH: AN OUTLINE

1 Commitments

1.1 The three styles of social research give different orders of priority to the range of methodological problems which face social scientists.

Before reading on I suggest that, on the basis of your reading in the course so far, you make notes on what you consider to be the main differences in approach between ethnography on the one hand, and experiments and surveys on the other. The rest of this first section will elaborate the distinctive features of ethnography.

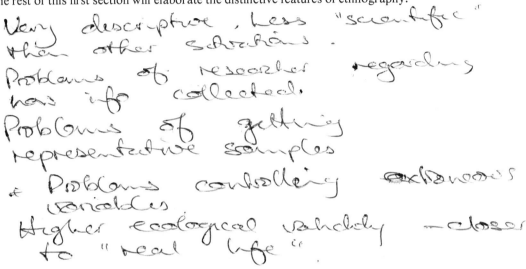

Very descriptive, less "scientific" than other solutions.
Problems of researcher regarding has info collected.
Problems of getting representative samples
+ Problems controlling extraneous variables
Higher ecological validity — closer to "real life".

1.2 Ethnography has been much more concerned with the problems of *description* and *ecological validity* than have been the other styles (see Block 3, Part 1). Indeed, ethnographers regard experimental and survey research as generally failing to take sufficient account of these problems. But, as is often the case in such matters, the strategies used by ethnographers to try to cope more adequately with these issues make the problems of *representation* and *control* more difficult to deal with.

description
Block 3, Part 1,
para. 1.12–1.15

representation,
control

1.3 In ethnography, research design refers to a multitude of decisions that have to be taken *over the whole course of the fieldwork*. In each case the strategy that is adopted depends to a great extent on the nature of the social situation chosen for study. There can, therefore, be no single ideal to which all such research can be expected to conform. However, ethnography does provide a set of general commitments or orientations to research which is rather different from those of the experimental and survey styles. These can be identified as:

(a) The problem of understanding social action (*understanding and interpretation*).

(b) The emphasis on process (*process*).

(c) The investigation of 'natural' settings (*naturalism*).

(d) The study of social phenomena in their context (*holism*).

(e) The assumption that there are always multiple perspectives (*multiple perspectives*).

Understanding and Interpretation

1.4 The social world differs from the natural world because it is *essentially* a world of interpretations and meanings. (This argument has already been introduced in Block 1, Part 3, in connection with the notion of explanation-by-understanding. Ball, in the article which was set reading for Block 1, shows how people's perceptions of legality and morality affected what they did in the abortion clinic.) People differ from natural objects in their ability to interpret their own actions and those of others, to act on their understandings and to endow their lives and actions with meaning. The social world of a particular culture is, therefore, *socially constructed*; it is the active accomplishment of the members of that culture. For this reason the language of ethnography refers to *actors* and *actions*, rather than, say, 'subjects' and 'behaviour', and the question is always 'how is it done?': 'what cultural resources, stocks of knowledge, routines and strategies do the actors bring to bear?'; 'how do the actors collectively negotiate and achieve social order, understanding and working relationships?'.

Block 1, Part 3, section 8

social construction
actor, action

1.5 *Action* is seen as purposive and meaningful, rather than totally determined by 'social structures', 'drives', 'environment' or 'social pressures'.[1] This is in direct contrast to the view that social phenomena can only be studied scientifically as objects which are causally related to one another in exactly the same ways as are physical objects.

Max Weber

George Herbert Mead

Process

1.6 Ethnographers argue that meanings and interpretations are not fixed entities. They are generated through social interaction and may change over the course of interaction. Actors' identities are also subject to processes of 'becoming' rather than being fixed and static. No single meaning or identity is assumed: there are multiple and competing definitions current in almost every social situation. The metaphor of *negotiation* is often used to capture the *processes* of interaction whereby social meanings are generated, and a precarious social order is produced. The recent history of the sociology of education in Britain illustrates this commitment.

negotiation

[1] *This notion of action is primarily associated with the sociological traditions deriving from Max Weber and George Herbert Mead. It is also an element of some varieties of social and clinical psychology. Kelly's theory of personal constructs, for example, emphasizes how people construct and interpret their own personal 'worlds' (Kelly, 1955; Shotter, 1975).*

Only recently have sociologists of education begun ethnographic research on classroom interaction

1.7 Until the 1960s sociological research in the area of education all too often treated the school as a 'black box': researchers were generally content to measure the 'input' (e.g. social class, family background and individual ability) and the 'output' (e.g. attainment and occupation), whilst the process of schooling remained largely unexplored. The Plowden research represents this kind of approach. You will remember how Bernstein and Davies (1969) (set reading for Block 1, Part 2) noted that Plowden makes little attempt at detailed description of schools and pointed to its 'trivial' discussion of differences in schools, justified by the claim that 'what goes on in primary schools cannot greatly differ from one school to another, since there is only a limited range of material within the capacity of primary school children' (Bernstein and Davies, 1969, p. 72). Since the 1960s there has been increasing (though still fairly limited) research into school life and the process of schooling. In Britain this received its initial impetus from researchers working in the anthropological tradition (Hargreaves, 1967; Lacey, 1970). Since then sociologists of education have begun to study the process of schooling and, in particular, face-to-face interaction in classrooms. Typical concerns have been the development of pupil identities, teachers' perceptions of pupils and their abilities, the 'management' of classroom knowledge, pupils' definitions of school subjects and so on. (Examples of such work are collected in Stubbs and Delamont, 1975 and Woods and Hammersley, 1977.)

Naturalism

1.8 Ethnographers recognize that what people say and do depends on the social context in which they find themselves. They urge, therefore, that social life be studied as it occurs, in *natural* settings rather than 'artificial' ones created only for the purposes of the research. Furthermore, they do not seek to manipulate and control what goes on in these settings but rather to minimize their own impact on events so as to be able, as far as possible, to observe social processes as they occur naturally without the intervention of researchers. Their aim is thereby to maximize the *ecological validity* of their findings. To some extent, therefore, ethnographers share a similar commitment with those ethologists who insist on the observation of animal life 'in the wild' and who argue against extrapolation from the unnatural conditions of captivity.

naturalism

ecological validity

Holism

1.9 Those working in the ethnographic tradition also stress the need to see social life within the general context of a culture, subculture or organization as a whole. The actions of individuals are motivated by events within the larger whole and thus cannot be understood apart from it. This *holistic* approach was of central importance in the development of social anthropology. Theorists of the nineteenth century tended to focus upon isolated aspects of culture (rituals, beliefs, etc.) and treat them out of their social context. (A classic example was Sir James Frazer's *The Golden Bough*[2].) These bits and pieces were fitted together into comparative

holism

James Frazer

[2] *James Frazer (1854–1941) was a very important figure in the establishment of anthropology as a subject. In his classic work* The Golden Bough *he sought to reconstruct the whole history of human thought, ordering a vast range of exotic beliefs and customs in terms of man's search for true knowledge and control over his environment. He had little or no contact with the peoples of whom he wrote, relying on the reports of travellers, missionaries etc. As a result he was not able to take into account the social context of the customs and beliefs with which he was concerned and he frequently misinterpreted them, forcing them into his evolutionary framework.*

Bronislaw Malinowski

and evolutionary schemes which rested upon the supposedly 'primitive' and 'superstitious' nature of non-western societies. Early fieldworkers such as Malinowski[3], on the other hand, emphasized the need to look at 'primitive' societies as functioning wholes. They therefore concentrated their attention on how the various elements of a culture fitted together to produce a coherent and functioning unity.

Multiple Perspectives

1.10 These early anthropological ethnographers also argued that 'savages' were not simply 'superstitious' or mentally inferior to western observers but rather employed *different*, equally rational, 'world-views'. Contemporary ethnographic approaches take a similar view and, rather than imposing their own modes of rationality on those they study, attempt to comprehend social action in terms of the actors' own terms of reference. As a result they are well-suited to the detection

[3] *Bronislaw Malinowski (1884–1942) is claimed by British social anthropologists, many of whom were his students, to have been the founding father of ethnographic fieldwork. While there had previously been expeditions by anthropologists to 'primitive' societies, these had usually involved only a brief stay and the primary concern had been the collection of specimens: cultural objects, accounts of rituals etc. Malinowski revolutionized fieldwork by stressing the importance of living among the natives for long periods of time and learning their language rather than relying on interpreters.*

of 'unofficial' versions of social reality. What people *do* and what they *ought* to do are very often different. Because of this there is frequently a discrepancy between what people *do* and what they *say* they do (Deutscher, 1966). Therefore, one must look beyond the 'public' and 'official' versions of reality, in order to examine the unacknowledged or tacit understandings as well. Deviance poses the problem of 'words' and 'deeds' in a particularly obvious way.

Before reading on, remind yourself why Ball advocated an ethnographic approach to the study of criminal abortions. Look back at the article if necessary.

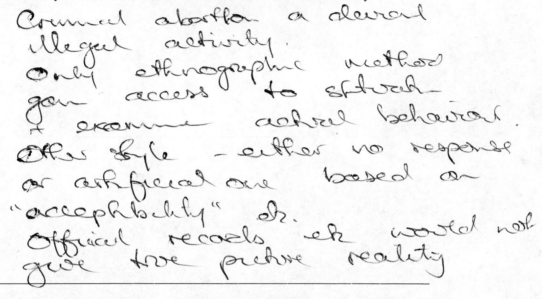

Criminal abortion a deviant illegal activity.
Only ethnographic method can access to situation & examine actual behaviour.
Other style - either no response or artificial one based on "acceptability" etc.
Official records etc would not give true picture reality

1.11 Ball suggests that deviance is not generally amenable to study via social surveys because respondents are likely to hide their involvement in deviant activities. He also points out that if the social scientist relies solely on official agencies and statistics concerning apprehended deviants, his data are open to *systematic* and often rather severe distortion of a number of sorts; for example, during a period when the police are subject to outside pressure to 'clean up the streets', we should expect a larger number of 'criminals' of certain types to be arrested. Furthermore, such a researcher will not arrive at any understanding of how deviants organize their activities, the culture of deviant groups and so on.

systematic error

1.12 The discrepancy between what is said to occur and what actually happens is not restricted to criminal activity however. It can be found in almost every setting. Thus, studies in education have highlighted 'unofficial' perspectives in a number of contexts, for example by drawing attention to the 'hidden curriculum'. This is the set of implicit messages and learning that go on in addition to, and sometimes in opposition to, the 'official' curriculum. A classic example of such an approach was undertaken by the authors of *Boys in white* (Becker, Geer, Hughes and Strauss, 1961) in which they documented in considerable detail the hidden curriculum of medical education at Kansas University.[4]

---

[4] *This is an example of the work of the Chicago School of American Sociology which was at its height in the 1930s but experienced a revival in the 1960s. Robert Park, Roderick McKenzie and Ernest Burgess were the most prominent members of the original Chicago School. In the earlier period it produced a large number of ethnographic studies of the underlife of the city (criminals, hobos, prostitutes, delinquents, bohemians). These studies were undertaken and presented from the point of view of the 'underdog', in an attempt to 'understand' them in their own terms and thereby counter the official bias which seemed to dominate many studies of such phenomena. Later the focus was extended beyond Chicago and to conventional occupational groups and educational settings.*

In participant observation research the fieldworker directly observes, and to some extent takes part in, everyday life in the setting

---

At this point you might find it useful to read the article by Becker and Geer, 'The fate of idealism in medical school'. It documents the way in which the idealistic attitudes the students have on entry to the medical school come to be replaced by a more pragmatic, cynical attitude which they generate to cope with the demands that are made on them.

(This is recommended reading for this Part, and is optional.)

SAQ 1
By now you are probably beginning to see a number of *implications* of these five commitments (understanding, process, naturalism, holism, and multiple perspectives) *for research design*. You might find it helpful to make brief notes of these implications.
Spend no more than ten minutes on this activity.

1.13   Ethnographic 'fieldwork' is not a homogeneous method, but involves a variety of techniques of data collection. The most commonly employed approach is that of *participant observation* whereby the fieldworker directly observes, and to some extent takes part in, everyday life in a chosen setting (a school, prison, bureaucracy, rural community, adolescent gang, etc.). Observations are recorded in the form of detailed *field-notes*, which may be made on the spot and amplified subsequently, or written up as soon as possible after leaving *the field*. In recent years audio and video-tape recordings have been increasingly used to obtain permanent records of social interaction. In addition the ethnographer may engage in interviewing, the collection and analysis of documentary material, and may also use the techniques of survey research to supplement the field-notes.

participant observation

field-notes

see section 10

2   Progressive Focusing: Formulating Problems and Testing Hypotheses

2.1   The generation and development of theories is a much more central concern in ethnographic research than it is in the other styles, where the emphasis is more on theory testing. Ethnographers are particularly concerned that their theories adequately capture the reality they are meant to explain. Formulating testable propositions is not, in itself, difficult. Finding *appropriate* research problems, finding the *right* questions to ask, most certainly are. It may be unproductive to ask a particular question at a particular stage in the development of a research field: for example because it is possible to answer it, or satisfactorily reformulate it, only after other questions have been answered. A case in point is the Plowden research which, in my view, quite begged the question of the nature of 'academic attainment' and the role of social interaction in its production including, for example, the effects of teachers labelling pupils 'bright' or 'thick'. The approach of ethnographers is *inductive* rather than deductive; they argue that the *hypothetico-deductive method* fails to deal with the question of how theories are generated and as a result those using this approach rely in an unsystematic way on their own personal experience to produce theoretical ideas. The danger in this is that the researcher will tend to impose his own commonsense ideas on the world, thereby prejudging important issues. In order to try to avoid this the ethnographer sets out to *generate* theory in a systematic and rigorous manner.

inductive procedure, hypothetico-deductive method

2.2   We can identify three broad phases in the development of fieldwork projects (Strauss *et al*, 1963):

(a)   *The initial phase*   Guided by broadly defined research interests, the fieldworker collects data with a view to trying out a wide range of possible ideas and lines of inquiry.

(b)   *The second phase*   Significant classes of persons and events begin to emerge. Initial research problems may have undergone reformulation, and ideas start to come into focus. Working hypotheses and propositions are formulated with reference to specific aspects of the field of study.

(c)   *The third phase*   The testing of a restricted number of hypotheses is undertaken.

At this point you might find it useful to read the article 'The research web', by Jaqueline Wiseman, which nicely illustrates the constant interplay of data gathering and analysis in ethnographic research.

(This article is recommended reading for this Part, and is optional.)

2.3   The guiding principle of ethnographic fieldwork, at least in the early stages, is 'learning'. The researcher tries to adopt the role of 'acceptable incompetent' (Lofland, 1971). The stance adopted is one of a radically naive observer who does not take it on trust that 'everyone knows' what goes on in any given context. By watching, listening and asking questions, the ethnographer comes to assimilate the knowledge and perspectives of the actors concerned. His general approach is not unlike that of all new recruits, novices and 'outsiders', except that he remains aware of the process of learning and develops such self-awareness as a resource in data collection and analysis; this is termed '*reflexivity*'.

reflexivity

2.4   The emphasis on discovery requires research strategies with a wide focus, collecting any data which are possibly relevant. Ethnographers try to avoid sharpening their problems into specific research hypotheses until considerable exploratory investigation has occurred (a process termed *progressive focusing*). This is another facet of the attempt to avoid commitment to existing theoretical and/or commonsense categories or sources of data: the data we collect in this exploratory fashion should give us some clues as to how best to formulate our research questions.

progressive focusing

2.5   This is not to suggest that ethnographers enter the field without guiding principles, with empty minds. Besides the general commitments we discussed in section 1, they generally begin with a broadly defined problem area and some *sensitizing concepts* drawn from previous research. Such problems can take two basic forms: they may be *topical*, relating to those categories, occasions and situations which are recognized commonsensically by actors, or *generic*, of a more abstract character and applying to a wide variety of topical problems. Examples of topical questions would be 'what are the critical features of academic study as experienced by students?' or 'how do machine operatives experience their work?'

sensitizing concept, topical problem, generic problem

Can you think what generic problems might be relevant to these two topical questions? For the first think of your own experience with DE304!

— machine workers — coping with boredom

— students effects studying done at home.

2.6   One suggestion is that the topical situation of the student may be viewed as an instance of open-ended and never-ending tasks which have to be made manageable. The situation of the machine-operator can be treated as an instance of the generic problem of monotony and how to deal with it (Lofland, 1977). An ethnographer may begin from a single substantive topic and draw on, or develop, a number of different generic concepts. Equally, however, the starting-point may be a generic problem, for example the problems of uncertainty and luck in work, the researcher selecting relevant empirical instances which may be expected to exemplify the concept: for example, professional sportsmen, confidence tricksters, surgeons, etc.

The experience of the machine operator can be treated as an instance of the generic problem of monotony and how to deal with it

2.7 In the second phase of fieldwork the central concern is the *development* of the theory which is beginning to emerge. One of the techniques ethnographers use in this task is *theoretical sampling*: in the light of emergent hypotheses the fieldworker seeks out new cases (settings, groups or individuals) in order to develop, test, modify and extend the hypotheses, and the concepts in terms of which they are expressed. Theoretical sampling differs from the method of *statistical sampling* to which you have been introduced earlier in this Block (Part 4) in a number of ways.

theoretical sampling

statistical sampling

Statistical Sampling	Theoretical Sampling
Performed on the basis of categories which are taken as given.	The purpose is to discover and develop categories.
Usually a one-off exercise to identify the targets for the data collection exercise.	A recurrent process in which at a number of points in the fieldwork samples are chosen which seem most likely to develop the theory.
Once the sample has been drawn every case in that sample must be investigated and analysed.	Cases are analysed only until new categories and properties are no longer appearing – to the point of what Glaser and Strauss call *theoretical saturation*.

theoretical saturation

2.8 Theoretical sampling involves the minimization and maximization of differences between comparison groups. The strategy of maximizing differences among comparison groups means that the researcher will find a very wide range of data bearing on a particular theme or concept. Minimizing differences between groups results in the researcher collecting a great deal of information bearing on a restricted range of phenomena; the variations that are consciously sought out will suggest modifications to the 'fine grain' of the developing hypothesis. Thus, by the selection of relevant comparison groups and by shifting the location of the fieldwork, the researcher can vary and *control* the characteristics of people and situations. But here of course the purpose of controlled comparison is the generation and development of theory rather than theory testing.

2.9 The process is best illustrated by a concrete example. The formulation of theoretical sampling by Glaser and Strauss (1967) derives in part from their research on dying in hospitals. They were interested in the *awareness* of dying among terminally ill patients – a problem which led them to consider the processes of communication and deception between patients, their families and hospital staff. To indicate the flavour of theoretical sampling in such a study, Glaser and Strauss cite the following research memorandum (that is, a note prepared in the course of a project in which the researcher makes explicit the developing lines of thought and fieldwork strategies):

> Visits to the various medical services were scheduled as follows: I wished first to look at services that minimized patient awareness (and so first looked at a premature baby service and then a neurosurgical service where patients were frequently comatose). I wished next to look at dying in a situation where expectancy of staff and often of patients was great and dying was quick, so I observed on an Intensive Care Unit. Then I wished to observe on a service where staff expectations of terminality were great but where the patient's might or might not be, and where dying tended to be slow. So I looked next at a cancer service. I wished then to look at conditions where death was unexpected and rapid, and so looked at an emergency service. While we were looking at some different types of services, we also observed the above types of service at other types of hospitals. So our scheduling of types of service was directed by a general conceptual scheme – which included hypotheses about awareness, expectedness and rate of dying – as well as by a developing conceptual structure including matters not at first envisioned. Sometimes we returned to services after the initial two or three of four weeks of continuous observation, in order to check upon items which needed checking or had been missed in the initial period. (Glaser and Strauss, 1967, p. 59)

2.10 Incidentally, it is worth noting that Glaser and Strauss originally conceived of their research as a study of the management of dying – a *topical* problem area. They then proceeded to identify several *generic* approaches which illuminate the process. For instance, they saw that it had affinities with other *status passages* (such as birth, marriage, initiation ceremonies); they also analysed it from the perspective of the social distribution of knowledge and awareness (developing the notion of *awareness contexts*); this links the topic with other situations in which actors try to perserve or break down conditions of secrecy and pretence. They thereby developed theories about two generic problems.

status passage

awareness context

2.11 Theoretical sampling is one form of the *comparative method*. In the third phase of fieldwork the central concern is testing the theory that has been developed. Here again there is a reliance on controlled comparison, in this case as an alternative to the use of physical and statistical controls which, in general, are not available to ethnographers. What we must do if we are to examine the relationship between phenomena is to select situations which differ in known ways and compare them on other dimensions. In this way we may be able to *approximate* the conditions of controlled experiments so that we can employ the 'all other things being equal' assumption. In order to test their theories, then, ethnographers sometimes use another form of the comparative method known as *analytic induction*. (This bears important similarities to Popper's general approach of conjectures and refutations. See Block 1, Part 3.) Described abstractly it involves the following steps:

comparative method

analytic induction
Block 1, Part 3,
paras. 7.7–7.11

(a)   A rough description of the general phenomenon to be explained is formulated as a result of the researcher's explorations of a small number of particular cases.

(b)   A hypothetical explanation of the phenomenon is formulated; often several competing explanations are developed.

(c)   Each of a small number of new cases (sometimes from the same setting, sometimes from different settings) is studied in light of the hypothesis, with the object of determining whether or not the hypothesis explains that case.

(d)   If the hypothesis does not explain that case, either the hypothesis is reformulated or the phenomenon to be explained is redefined so that the case is excluded.

(e)   In the selection of new cases, the researcher is explicitly recommended to maximize the chances of discovering negative cases in order to highlight critical deficiencies in the ideas under exploration.

(f)   This procedure of examining cases, redefining the phenomenon, and reformulating the hypotheses is continued until no further counter-examples are encountered, and all sources of likely negative evidence have been explored.

> Lindesmith's (1947, 1968) research on opiate addiction provides an illustration of this method. The focus of his investigation was the development of a sociological theory of opiate addiction. He began with the tentatively formulated hypothesis that individuals who did not know what drug they were receiving would not become addicted. Conversely, it was predicted that individuals would become addicted when they knew what they were taking, and had taken it long enough to experience withdrawal distress when they stopped. This hypothesis was destroyed when one of the first addicts interviewed, a doctor, stated that he had once received morphine for several weeks, was fully aware of the fact, but had not become addicted at that time. This negative case, forced Lindesmith to reformulate his initial hypothesis to state:

Persons become addicts when they recognize or perceive the significance of withdrawal distress which they are experiencing, and that if they do not recognize withdrawal distress they do not become addicts regardless of any other considerations [1947, p. 8].

This formulation proved to be much more powerful, but again negating evidence forced its revision. In this case persons were observed who had withdrawal experiences and understood withdrawal distress, but not in the most severe form; these persons did not use the drug to alleviate the distress and never became addicts. Lindesmith's final causal hypothesis involved a shift on his part from the recognition of withdrawal distress, to the use of the drug after this insight had occurred for the purposes of alleviating the distress [1947, p. 8].

This final hypothesis had the advantage of attributing the cause of addiction to no single event, but to a complex chain of events. The final hypothesis, which in reality represented a chain of propositions, involved the following:

1   Addiction rests fundamentally upon the effects which follow when the drug is removed, rather than on the positive effects which its presence in the body produces.

2   Addiction occurs only when opiates are used to alleviate withdrawal distress, after this distress has been properly understood or interpreted. That is, after it has been represented to the individual in terms of linguistic symbols and cultural patterns which have grown up around the opiate habit.

3   If the individual fails to conceive of his distress as withdrawal distress brought about by the absence of opiates, he cannot become addicted, but if he does, addiction is quickly and permanently established through further use of the drug [1947, p. 165].

All of the evidence unequivocally supported the above theory, and Lindesmith concluded:

This theory furnishes a simple but effective explanation, not only of the manner in which addiction becomes established, but also of the essential features of addiction behaviour, those features which are found in addiction in all parts of the world, and which are common to all cases [1947, p. 165].

Before reaching the conclusion that his theory explained all cases of opiate addiction, Lindesmith explicitly searched for negative cases that would force revision or rejection of the theory. He describes this process as follows:

Each succeeding tentative formulation was not constructed *de novo*, but was based upon that which had preceded it. The eventual hypothesis altered the preceding formulations sufficiently to include the cases which earlier had appeared as exceptions to the theory postulated.

It may be asked whether the search for negative cases was properly conducted and if the observer has not neglected evidence of a contradictory character. To this, of course, there is no final answer. It is probable that somewhere in the course of any study unconscious distortion takes place. Concerning the central hypothesis and the direct lines of evidence, however, certain procedures were followed which may be said to exclude bias. For example, when the theory had been stated in an approximation of its final form it occurred to the writer that it could be tested in cases where an individual had had two separate experiences with morphine or opiates, each of which was sufficiently prolonged to produce withdrawal distress but with addiction following only the second episode. Case 3 in Chapter Four is an example. It was concluded that if the theory was valid, the person would report that he had failed to realize the nature of withdrawal in that experience from which he had escaped without becoming addicted. Thereupon a thorough search was made for cases in which an individual had undergone such an experience with the drug prior to becoming an addict. All cases of this kind which could be found, or of which any record could be located, were taken into account. Any of these cases might have contradicted the final hypothesis, but none did so. The inference or prediction which had been drawn on the basis of the theory was fully borne out. This procedure was followed throughout the study wherever possible . . . [1947, pp. 9–10]. (Denzin, 1970, pp. 195–7)

2.12   The comparative method may also be used after fieldwork has been completed where what is compared are the results of many different fieldwork projects. Goody (1976) provides an example of this from social anthropology. In the course of his own fieldwork among two neighbouring communities in West Africa he became interested in modes of inheritance and their implications for systems of kinship and marriage (the two communities provided the basis for a small-scale comparison). In later studies Goody elaborated a number of hypotheses concerning relationships between patterns of inheritance and systems of agriculture, dealing specifically with the change from hoe to plough agriculture. He has gone on to elaborate and test these hypotheses by analysing a wide range of cross-cultural data drawn from Africa and Eurasia. The data are taken from a computer file known as the *Ethnographic Atlas* in which are coded the findings of a large number of ethnographies; it thus provides a major source for the analysis of secondary material. There are problems in using this source (the reports used are not equally trustworthy, for instance), but it provides a way of trying to test a number of propositions cross-culturally in a methodical way.

2.13   The comparative method also allows us to document the range of variation in human behaviour. This is a valuable antidote to premature generalization. For instance, cross-cultural data on sex roles suggests that there is nothing in human behaviour that is inherently and universally 'masculine' or 'feminine'. This comparative perspective thus helps us guard against '*ethnocentrism*' – that is, judging all human action from the standpoint of our own culture.

ethnocentrism

2.14   *Summary*   The preceding paragraphs have outlined some of the commitments (theoretical and methodological) of ethnography, and the logic of discovery that it entails. What the fieldworker actually *does* may seem similar to everyday activity, but, unlike the 'layman', he or she remains self-conscious and preserves a permanent, retrievable record. The ethnographic method also differs from 'lay' observation and interpretation insofar as the researcher does not simply gather a mass of impressions but rather collects data in a systematic and principled way; that is, in accordance with a theoretical framework and in the light of hypotheses which are developed and made explicit in the course of fieldwork. The procedures of the comparative method – theoretical sampling and analytic induction – provide strategies for such a methodical approach.

B: PRE-FIELDWORK

3   The Research Setting

3.1   Ethnographers normally study only a single setting, or a small number of settings at one time. There is a trade-off between depth and breadth of coverage; the limitations of time and labour often preclude the exhaustive investigation of many different settings or locales within the same research project. The nature of the chosen research setting(s) is therefore crucial. A recurrent question for ethnographic research is: 'was the setting of the research typical of its sort?'

To which of the 'tensions' discussed in Part 1 of this Block does this question relate?

Mainly of typicality and representativeness.

Block 3, Part 1, Figure 1, and paras 1.12–1.15

3.2   What is involved in the ethnographic concern with the 'typicality' of a setting is the 'population – sample' tension (i.e. the problem of *representation*).

3.3   *Typicality*   The search for 'typical' settings is by no means straightforward. As we have seen already, the focus of the research is an emergent one, and the formulation of specific problems often cannot be completed prior to the fieldwork itself. Hence notions of *typicality* in the selection and reporting of research sites can all too easily beg important questions – anticipating what should be the *outcome* of the research project. Let us suppose, for instance, that we were planning to undertake a study of a mental hospital. We might well have in mind the *generic problem* of 'total institutions'[5] (Goffman, 1968), and we might wish to ask whether our mental hospital was going to be a typical case of a total institution.

Erving Goffman

[5] *Goffman developed this concept in connection with his study of the social situation of mental patients and extended it to the situations experienced by inmates of prisons, military camps, and monasteries. He defines a total institution as 'a place of residence and work where a large number of like-situated individuals, cut off from the wider society for an appreciable period of time, together lead an enclosed, formally administered round of life' (Goffman, 1968, p. 11).*

In order to plan the research from that point of view, what prior information would we need?

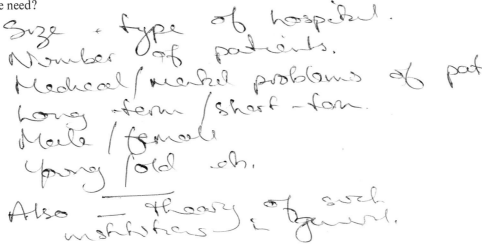

Size + type of hospital.
Number of patients.
Medical/mental problems of patients.
Long term/short-term.
Male/female
Young/old etc.

Also — theory of such
institutions i general.

3.4 In order to *plan* the research from that point of view, we should need to have (a) a fully developed theory of total institutions, and (b) a detailed knowledge of the organization and everyday working of the hospital in question. Even if we had a definitive theory, the second requirement would still assume that the study had been completed, not that it was in the planning stage.

3.5 Of course, one can usefully employ criteria to establish a number of basic characteristics of a 'field'. For instance, in selecting a school or schools, in order, say, to describe the nature of 'educational attainment' and the way it is produced one might bear in mind such features as its size, catchment area, method of selection (if any), streaming policy, whether it was single sex or mixed, whether there was any religious affiliation, etc. Such characteristics would be noted as a matter of course as *potentially* useful, but could not be guaranteed to be relevant to the topical and generic problems under investigation.

3.6 The amount of information that can be gleaned beforehand in the selection of a research site varies widely. Formal organizations normally have well-defined characteristics (lists of members, stated policies, formal rules) which may be available to the researcher. Less formal groupings will not be documented in the same way, and the characteristics may be far less easy to specify at the outset. (Note, however, that ethnographers do not necessarily adopt these characteristics as the exclusive conceptual framework for their work; for these characteristics do not necessarily correspond to the notions employed by the actors under investigation to make sense of their own *social worlds*.)

3.7 However, research settings may prove fruitful precisely because they are not typical, or do not fit an expected pattern. The exploration of unusual or extreme examples may help to illuminate more general features – throwing them into sharp relief, casting doubt on cherished, taken-for-granted ideas, and pushing existing theories and concepts to the limits of their application. The close examination of the unusual case can highlight aspects of the 'typical' and the 'routine' which might otherwise pass unnoticed as 'obvious' and 'normal', and hence unremarkable. 'Deviant' or *critical case analysis* thus plays an important part in the generation of hypotheses and testing them in different contexts (cf. the outline of the comparative method, paragraph 2.11 above).

critical case analysis

3.8 Goffman's work on mental hospitals is a good example of using extreme cases to show up features of the mundane. In examining the lives of mental patients he showed the importance for their self-conceptions of apparently trivial matters such as having to ask attendants for a light for cigarettes, with the possibility of being refused; or the significance of having to wear standardized, ill-fitting hospital clothes.

3.9 The choice of a particular setting may be prompted by a period of *change and innovation* in that setting. The process of innovation may be studied for its own sake, or may be used to highlight other concerns. During periods of change and upheaval actors may need to question their beliefs and their taken-for-granted views of themselves and the social world. It may therefore prove a fruitful strategy deliberately to select fields for research in which innovatory processes are taking place. Thus, for instance, there have been ethnographic studies of the institution of new curricula in schools, such as those sponsored by the Schools Council (one recent example is Shipman *et al*, 1974). Here the emphasis on the 'unofficial' plays an important part. Although such changes are directed towards specific aims and objectives, there are always unintended consequences; no new curriculum can be guaranteed to be 'child-proof' or 'teacher-proof'. Thus it becomes extremely important that investigators should trace the day-to-day processes of change and its unforeseen consequences (cf. Hamilton, 1976; MacDonald and Walker, 1976).

3.10 Once a setting for the research has been identified it may be subjected to a preliminary examination that Schatzman and Strauss (1973) call *casing*. This is undertaken in order to appraise the research potential and in order to assess the practicalities of data collection. Schatzman and Strauss (p. 19) identify three major objectives for casing:

casing

(a)   To determine as precisely as possible whether this site does, in fact, meet his requirements – a question of *suitability*.

(b)   To 'measure' some of its presenting properties (size, spatial scatter, etc.) against his own resources of time, mobility, skills and whatever else it would take to do the job – a question of *feasibility*.

(c)   To gather information about the place and people there in preparation for negotiating entry – a question of *tactics*.

Such 'casing' may be done from a distance, using sources such as handbooks, prospectuses, official reports, or one may use informal social contacts prior to more formal moves in gaining access.

4   Constituting the Field

4.1 The vocabulary of 'the field' and 'entering the field' is widely used in writing and talking about ethnography; similarly, the terminology often includes reference to 'social worlds' (see paragraph 3.6). These are short-hand terms to describe the experience of research in this style. Yet they carry their own dangers. They have connotations of self-contained, neatly bounded groups or milieux. To the unwary – and even to the experienced – they can suggest a ready-packaged set of actors, locales and activities which present themselves for observation and analysis. One can, therefore, be drawn into a search for self-contained groups, communities or organizations. The prospect of establishing such research settings may appear attractive, offering readily manageable 'slices of life' which can easily be encompassed by the personal involvement of a fieldworker or team of fieldworkers. Such a view may be reinforced by a commitment to treat social life holistically rather than dealing with isolated phenomena.

4.2 It is certainly the case that some groups and organizations are more self-contained than others – those that Goffman (1968) calls 'total institutions' for instance. But the fieldworker should not predetermine that very issue by limiting

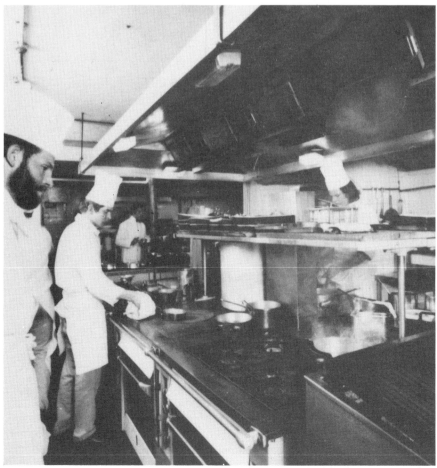

Hotels, like many other settings, have backstage and frontstage regions.

the scope of the research unduly. Nor should he suppose that the boundaries he has set on his research – for example, studying pupils within school, but not their out-of-school lives – actually represent features of the world as experienced by the actors he is studying. While pupils will probably make a distinction between 'in' school and 'out', they may draw the distinction differently to the researcher – for example, by including the journey to and from school as in-school, or they may lump together being at school and at home and contrast it as with being 'out with the gang'. Thus an undue emphasis on self-contained 'fields' may involve precisely the sort of question-begging and imposition of conceptual schemes which ethnographers seek to avoid. Demographic and organizational boundaries should not be incorporated uncritically into research designs.

4.3 'Fields', then, are not naturally occurring categories or phenomena which exist 'out there'; they are themselves socially constructed. Participants normally recognize a range of different arenas or *social contexts* which are associated with notions of 'legitimate membership' and 'appropriate activities'. For instance, Goffman (1971) describes the distinction between 'backstage' and 'frontstage' settings in a hotel. From the perspective of the hotel staff, the 'backstage' regions (staff quarters, kitchens, etc.) are private, whereas they confront the hotel guests in public dealings in 'frontstage' regions. The demeanour appropriate and permissible in these two regions differs markedly, and the invasion of the backstage by hotel guests would constitute a major breach of the social boundary between them. But such boundaries are not absolutely fixed. They are produced and sustained by actors' own definitions, and are therefore available for negotiation and redefinition. The researcher has to locate the ethnographic enterprise with reference to these *member-identified* settings (see paragraph 9.7). The researcher's own presence, sense of place and developing membership are, therefore, gained in relation to the participants' own shared sense of the 'field'.

social context

see para. 9.7

SAQ 2
At this point, consider an organization with which you are, or have been, familiar. Note down two or three different social settings, 'regions' or contexts within it. How do they differ in terms of their membership and the activities appropriate to them?
Spend no more than fifteen minutes on this activity. You might like to turn to the end of this Part to compare your thoughts with my notes on a department store where I used to work.

4.4 The ethnographer, then, must not mistake the field of research he adopts for a real-world phenomenon. Indeed one of the aspects of the social world he must seek to discover is the boundaries that members establish and maintain in their interactions with one another.

5   Familiarity and Strangeness

5.1 It is often tempting to choose a research setting in which you already play a role – on the basis of employment or voluntary membership. This recourse has a number of attractions and a number of drawbacks.

Spend a minute or two noting two or three advantages and two or three disadvantages of work in a familiar setting. You will find some of them discussed in paragraph 5.2 onwards.

Already have knowledge – less preparatory work necessary. Likely know + have some 'real life' images of institution. Already accepted + member.

Might overlook many actions + processes by assumption + familiarity

May interact differently with others due to new role.

5.2   In the first instance, one already enjoys *access* to the field. One's presence is legitimate (though not for the purpose of research). It may be possible to use prior membership as a resource in negotiating permission and facilities to carry out the research. Secondly, there will be networks of colleagues and friends; they may be drawn on in the collection of information. Thirdly, prior involvement in the field can short-cut some of the time-consuming and stressful aspects of fieldwork in novel settings. One will have a stock of background information, a 'working knowledge' of routine tasks and troubles. Similarly, any special technical information or jargon will probably be familiar.

access

5.3   On the other hand, ethnographers aim to make everyday life 'anthropologically strange'. That is, they treat as problematic things that actors themselves treat as normal. Even in unfamiliar settings this may call for a considerable effort of self-awareness and imagination. For instance, Geer (1964) remarks that 'Untrained observers . . . can spend a day in a hospital and come back with one page of notes and no hypotheses. It was a hospital, they say; everyone knows what hospitals are like'. As you can imagine, it is even more difficult to distance oneself as a well-established participant. Over-familiarity can deprive a researcher of a valuable resource: the cutting edge of 'strangeness' is dulled.

5.4   Furthermore, the well-established member will be involved in existing patterns of social interaction, influence and authority. It may prove difficult during fieldwork to keep a distance from one's own interest group, faction or clique. Free social movement among other groups may therefore be impaired.

5.5   The attempt to be both a member and a researcher can often lead to problems of *role conflict*. (The researcher's role will be more fully discussed in section 8.) This is well illustrated by Hargreaves (1967, Appendix). In the course of his study of a boys' secondary school, Hargreaves worked as a teacher. In doing so he believed that he would demonstrate to the teachers that he was willing and able to see things from their point of view, and that he was not a 'spy' from the education authority. But as soon as he turned from teaching to data collection in other teachers' classrooms this conflicted with the normal behaviour expected

role conflict
see section 8

63

of colleagues. They saw him as a sort of school Inspector and his relations with them were compromised. His participation with the pupils was also hampered by activities as a teacher and he was forced to abandon the teacher role. Hargreaves' difficulties also show how short-term strategies for gaining access or establishing a role in the field may in fact lead to long-term difficulties and place constraints on the collection of data.

6 Getting In

6.1 The identification of a locale for research is only the start of a complex process of 'getting in' and 'getting started'. Problems of access arise in most contexts, although they are not equally complex in all cases. Places and situations differ in the extent to which they are 'open' to observation.

SAQ 3

Listed below are the authors and subject matter of a number of ethnographic studies which appear in the same reader, *People in places* (Birenbaum and Sagarin, 1973). Consider:

(a) how open to investigation each of the places would have been;

(b) what, if any, special problems of access might have confronted the researchers.

(i) Michael Wolff, 'Notes on the behaviour of pedestrians' (observations on Forty-Second Street, New York).

(ii) Janey Levine, Anne Vinson and Deborah Wood, 'Subway behaviour' (observations on New York and Boston underground).

(iii) Sherri Cavan, 'Bar sociability' (observations in San Francisco bars).

(iv) William Foote Whyte, 'The social structure of the restaurant' (twelve Chicago restaurants).

Spend no more than ten minutes on this.

6.2 In organizations, official agencies and so on there are individuals who, by virtue of their office, have the authority to act as *gatekeepers*. They can grant or withhold formal permission to enter and participate in the life of the organization. Dealings with such gatekeepers can therefore be an extremely important part of the design and conduct of ethnography.

gatekeeper

6.3 Gatekeepers have a number of characteristic interests and perceptions of the research enterprise. They normally require some indication of the researcher's intentions. Fieldworkers should therefore be prepared to offer some outline proposal. This declaration of intent should be sufficiently broad as to allow the research to develop over time. It is not necessary (or desirable) to ask for everything from the outset. If there are likely to be sensitive issues or particularly private occasions, then it is often wise to avoid direct requests for access to them at the outset, to 'shelve' them until a secure position in the field has been established.

6.4 In presenting one's declaration of intent, either verbally or in writing, it is imperative that it make sense to the gatekeepers. This sounds obvious, but it is a common elementary pitfall to make initial approaches that are expressed in the vocabulary of the social sciences. It is also advisable to avoid giving any impression that the hosts will be subject to evaluation or criticism. It is therefore customary to present the study as some straightforward 'fact-finding' or preliminary exercise.

Gatekeepers, such as headmasters, can grant or withhold formal permission to enter a setting

---

SAQ 4

Read the following statements of research objectives (taken from Dean *et al*, 1967). Consider what might be wrong with them, and spend about ten minutes in composing alternative formulations of each which you think might go down better with gatekeepers. At the end of the Part you will find the alternatives suggested by Dean and his colleagues.

(a)   We want to study what makes for good and bad union leadership.

(b)   We want to learn what the roots of effective political organization are – how much patronage, hired help, volunteer help, etc. – figure in local party campaigns.

(c)   We are interested in racial tension, discriminations and prejudice and how they are related to each other in a community.

6.5   Gatekeepers are often wary of the proposed lengthy and intimate participation of the fieldworker; they normally seek reassurances that the research will not prove unduly disruptive; that is, that the fieldworker will not prevent people from getting on with their normal work, force an entry into private meetings or conversations and so on. Gatekeepers need to be reassured that relations of trust and confidentiality will not be abused; as in any variety of research, ethnographers have to ensure the anonymity of the members concerned and that nothing will be made public that is detrimental to individuals. These issues are particularly critical in the context of ethnography, since the actions and beliefs of actors will be documented in some detail, and ethnographers are more likely than most other researchers to see 'behind the scenes'. In the Appendix to this Part you will find reproduced a letter sent out in connection with a fieldwork project (Schatzman and Strauss, 1973). Here you will see how two experienced fieldworkers attempt to cope with gatekeepers' possible worries on these scores.

see Appendix

6.6   Gatekeepers often engage in *impression management*. Quite naturally, they do not want to find the ethnographer producing an unflattering portrait of them and their work or their organization. Consciously or unconsciously they will 'put on a show', attempting to influence the initial impressions the fieldworker receives. The fieldworker must remain alert to such possibilities and record them systematically, since they constitute valuable data in their own right – throwing light on the gatekeepers' perceptions and preoccupations.

impression management

SAQ 5

You might like to reflect on some social group, association or organization that you know. If you were acting as a gatekeeper would there be any aspects that you would try to 'play down' or 'play up' in your dealings with a potential researcher?

Spend no more than ten minutes working on this activity.

6.7   In the course of such 'impression management', gatekeepers are often found to attempt to steer the research in one direction or another. Bogdan and Taylor (1975) offer the following illustration of this:

> We know one novice who contacted a detention home in order to set up a time to begin his observation. The supervisor with whom he spoke told him that he wouldn't be interested in visiting the home that day or the next because the boys would just be making Hallowe'en decorations. He then suggested which times of the day would be best for the observer to 'see something going on'. The observer allowed himself to be forced to choose from a limited number of alternatives when he should have made it clear that he was interested in a variety of activities and times. (Bogdan and Taylor, 1975, p. 45)

Under ideal circumstances, the observer would have explained that he wished to observe even the most 'dull' and 'mundane' aspects of the boys' lives *and* would have treated the supervisor's reluctance as a potentially relevant piece of data. This problem often confronts experienced fieldworkers and is not confined to 'novices'.

6.8   The task of gaining access must not be seen simply as a more or less annoying preliminary to the real work of data collection. It is *integral* to it. Gatekeepers are significant members of any group or organization; what they say and do must therefore enter into any systematic study of it. The fieldworker must pay close attention to the gatekeepers' 'impression management' strategies:

What areas do they seem touchy and sensitive about? What do *they* seem to think are the important areas for investigation and assume that the researcher will be interested in? What areas of conflict do they seem to perceive? Do they seem to gloss over them? In general, what picture of themselves and their colleagues are the gatekeepers trying to promote?

6.9   At the same time, the ethnographer is engaged in strategies aimed at promoting a favourable impression of himself. One needs to take care with *self-presentation*, with one's dress and demeanour, in order to reassure gatekeepers that one will act responsibly, will not disrupt events, be unduly out of place and so on. Again, this sounds obvious, but it often requires a degree of conscious management. When I was negotiating access to some teaching hospitals I made an elementary blunder: I misinterpreted a formal interview as an informal meeting and appeared casually and thus inappropriately dressed. It took some considerable effort to repair the unfavourable impression I had inadvertently conveyed.

6.10   Most gatekeepers are not familiar with the ethnographic style of research. If they have any expectation of social research, the survey will probably be their model. Fieldworkers are often asked, therefore, to spell out their 'hypotheses' and to show their draft questionnaires or interview schedules. Given a commitment to progressive focusing and a flexible research strategy, it may be rather difficult to establish one's legitimacy as a social researcher. As has already been suggested it is often a good plan to work in strange surroundings. But ignorance of the field does not always go down well with the gatekeepers; it jars with commonsense notions of the 'expert' investigator. It is therefore often necessary to display an informed awareness of potential problems and disruptions, while at the same time expressing a willingness to 'learn the ropes' in the field.

6.11   Many research settings require negotiation with more than one gatekeeper and the fieldworker may have to pass through several levels or types of authority (e.g. heads of different departments, management and unions in industrial contexts). This too is a source of data. The researcher may pick up valuable clues as to differing perspectives which foreshadow possible lines of systematic comparison between different groups, factions, levels of authority and so on.

SAQ 6
A school classroom is a familiar setting for research and potentially requires negotiation with many gatekeepers. Spend no more than five minutes listing the various persons with whom a researcher might have to negotiate in order to gain access. You will find a list of possible gatekeepers in the answer at the end of the Part – although you should be aware that not every project will involve interaction with *all* of them.

6.12   The process of negotiation in the field is a continuous one and it does not stop once formal access has been granted. To the extent that anyone has the ability to decide whether or not to co-operate with the researcher, each person has to be negotiated with individually. Also, as new topics arise in the research the fieldworker may need to negotiate afresh with the same actors – to be admitted to a new range of situations (such as private occasions which were not open at the outset of the research).

6.13   Hitherto we have concentrated on gaining access to institutions or organizations where formal permission is sought. There are, however, many social milieux where entrance cannot be effected by such obvious routes. A great deal of ethnographic work has been done on aspects of 'underlife', on street corners, in bars and poolrooms, etc., and access to such 'fields' must usually be a less clear-cut process. Although informal leaders and potential sponsors may exist, they are not necessarily visible and accessible to the would-be researcher at the outset. Entry must often be achieved by informal means – depending, even, on chance meetings and acquaintances, although prior 'contacts' may also be used. Snowball sampling (discussed in Part 4) may be a very useful way of getting started in these situations.

Block 3, Part 4, para. 3.6

At this point you should read sections 4, 5 and 6 of the 'Methodological appendix' from *Street corner society* by W. F. Whyte. This illustrates the process of access in the development of a classic urban ethnography. As you read the extracts, you should note the stages through which Whyte went in gaining access to his chosen field, the social contacts he formed and how these contacts affected the research strategy. (An edited version of the 'Methodological appendix' is supplied as Supplementary Material; although sections 4, 5 and 6 only are Set Reading for this Part, it is recommended that you read the whole extract.)

Now read Whyte (1955)

6.14   *Summary*   In this section we have gone through some of the preliminary phases of ethnographic study. One aspect that must be emphasized is the fact that these preliminaries are integral parts of the research as a whole. Data collection starts from the outset. The fieldworker seeks to document all aspects of the research process. If this is not attempted, the research may be subject to all sorts of biases of which the researcher remains unaware and which he cannot assess.

7   The Point of Entry

7.1   Once a site for the research has been selected and access negotiated, there may still remain further decisions and negotiations to be made concerning the precise point of entry. This is a general problem and becomes most pertinent when considering research in a large-scale organization. In many cases, it is impracticable to try to achieve total coverage, particularly if the research is being carried out single-handed. Furthermore, each different *point of entry* may have its own advantage of access and dangers of bias.

point of entry

7.2   The problem therefore becomes one of *strategic entry and location* in the field. The would-be fieldworker must, therefore, scan the field in order to identify vantage points. As outlined in paragraph 3.10 the researcher will have *cased* the field in order to appraise its research potential. A similar process often termed *mapping* can take place after initial entry (Schatzman and Strauss, 1973). Drawing on documentary sources, interviews with key informants, or personal experience, the researcher aims to build up some preliminary sense of the range of social settings, the division of labour, spatial arrangements and so on. Schatzman and Strauss recommend a 'Cook's tour' in order to familiarize oneself with the physical layout, patterns of work, the nature of social interaction and likely sources of data in various locales. On the basis of such a cursory examination the researcher can then set about deciding upon specific points of entry and can select locales for the accumulation of more detailed information.

strategic location

Block 3, Part 5, para. 3.10

mapping

7.3   Such 'mapping' can be illustrated from my own research in the Edinburgh medical school (Atkinson, 1976). Blanket coverage of this large and complex organization was quite impossible and it was imperative that I select one or more strategic locations and points of entry. It was possible to gain some sense of the organization from published curricula and timetables and after I gained formal access, I was also able to engage in preliminary observations to 'map' the organization. I spent brief periods observing the students at work in laboratories and in dissecting rooms as well as holding informal conversations with students and staff.

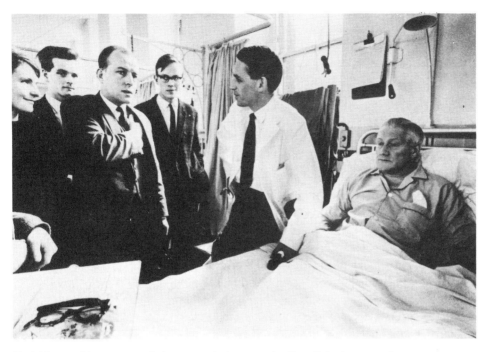

Bedside teaching – one of the central elements in the clinical years of medical education.

7.4 On the basis of these preliminaries I was able to pick on a suitable point of entry for the main data collection. It transpired that the transition from the 'pre-clinical' to the 'clinical' years marked a critical phase of the students' careers. The pre-clinical students saw this as a move towards the 'real' work of medicine, and the available literature reinforced the sense that the students' entry to the clinical years marked a significant turning point in their socialization. I therefore decided to focus my study on the students' introduction to clinical medicine. The subsequent fieldwork bore out this initial impression and it was possible to conduct a detailed investigation of a very important part of the organization as well as a particular phase of medical education.

SAQ 7
How many different points of entry can you think of in the case of a large car factory?

7.5 No less important is the *time* of entry. Pretty well every group, organization, social movement or whatever has its own rhythms, timetables and calendars. It may therefore be important to plan the timing of the research to take account of such timetables (e.g. the cycle of the school year). Particular periods of the social calendar can have great significance for actors. 'First days' are important: the 'reality shock' experienced by new recruits can be crucial in the formation of their perspectives and identities, and illuminating for the observer. At such times members are unable to take things for granted, and they have to work out solutions to their novel problems. At the same time, old hands may help them by making explicit what usually passes unnoticed.

7.6 Interest in such periods has to be set against the problem of *feasibility*. The key periods are significant precisely because routines are broken and established afresh. For this reason they are often treated as sensitive by gatekeepers and others. The first days of a new school year, for example, may be seen as such a 'delicate' period and observation discouraged until patterns of teaching and control have been established. If the preliminary formulation of the research problem suggests the potential value of observation at such times then it may be advisable to establish one's presence beforehand. In this way one may be able to maintain fieldwork into the more sensitive periods.

C: STRATEGIES IN THE FIELD

8 Field Roles

8.1 Participant observation requires sustained observation and interaction with 'hosts'. Hence the development of one's social role(s) in the field is central to the strategy of research design and data collection. It is not simply a personal concern, but is relevant to the validity of the findings. Ethnographers base their assumptions on the fact that social action depends upon the social context, and upon the mutual perceptions and understandings of the actors. If data are to be collected by means of first-hand involvement in the field, therefore, *reflexivity*, an explicit awareness of the ethnographer's own part in that social context, is a prerequisite to the evaluation and interpretation of the data. While the researcher aims at the unobtrusive, *naturalistic* study of social life, he or she also recognizes that the research act itself is part of the 'field' of study.

8.2 Part 3 of Block 4 will deal with *field roles* in more detail, and at this stage we simply introduce the topic. Gold (1958) describes four '*master roles*' that can be adopted in the course of fieldwork and they are identified by the degree of participation and involvement implied: **field role**   **master role**

(a) *The complete participant* operates under conditions of secret observation and full participation.

(b) *The complete observer* is entirely removed from interaction with those under observation.

Figure 1 Theoretical social roles for fieldwork

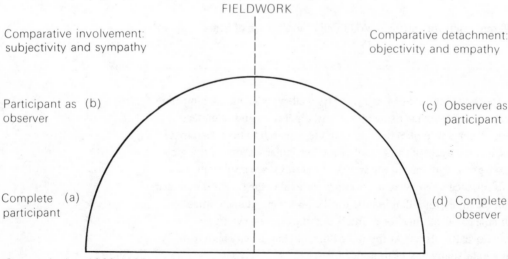

Source: Junker, 1960, p. 36

(c) *The observer as participant* is a role intermediate between the first two, where the researcher's identity is known to the hosts, but he or she remains a relative 'stranger'.

(d) *The participant as observer* is a similar role, but characterizes situations in which the fieldworker becomes more closely involved and identified with the actors.

The nature of these roles is summarized in Figure 1.

8.3 These 'master roles' gloss over a great diversity of social roles and interactional strategies that the fieldworker must engage in during a research project. They represent general orientations that may be adopted in the overall design and execution of the research. A consideration of the different available roles and their implications is a necessary part of the self-awareness that the ethnographer must cultivate. (These issues will be taken up in Block 4, Part 3.)

9 Sampling

9.1 Even when settings have been specified it is usually necessary to be more selective still. Even in fairly circumscribed social settings there will be too much going on for it all to be observed equally. As with other styles of research, therefore, *samples* must be drawn for detailed investigation and recording.

Can you think of some dimensions on the basis of which we ought to sample social interaction in a setting?

[handwritten: Criteria — Time, people & events]

9.2 We can identify three main criteria for sampling in the field – *time*, *people* and *events*. These will be discussed in turn.

Time

9.3 The social organization of time must be taken account of. Social activity differs at different times of the day, on different days of the week and at different times of the year. A study located in the casualty department of an inner city hospital, for instance, would have to take note of variations over time. Emergency admissions would almost certainly vary according to the time of day – related to the density of the traffic, pub closing times and so on. Saturday nights would be characterized not only by different rates but also by different types of admission from Sunday nights and so on.

9.4 In some contexts time may be formally organized – as in a factory shift system or a school timetable. In other settings time would be organized in more informal ways. In either event one cannot sustain field research round the clock and some attempt at sampling is necessary (although it is not unknown for people to do occasional periods of observation through twenty-four hours in order to cover the entire cycle of daily events: this would be a useful preliminary to the study of the casualty department, for instance). Rather than trying to cover the whole working day one can achieve a more manageable coverage by some sampling procedure. To begin with, long stretches of time may be spent in acquiring an extended, but fairly superficial sense of the action. One might perhaps observe the day shift for a few days, and then spend a few days with the night shift. More detailed coverage may then be achieved by observing overlapping periods – 7 a.m. to 9 p.m. on the first day, 8 a.m. to 10 p.m. on the second day and so on. Some particular periods will probably turn out to be critical (e.g. particularly busy or slack times, the change-over between shifts, the first and last periods of the school day and so on). These will be focused on for special attention. Carefully planned presence in the field will also provide for the sampling of weekly or seasonal variation (as with the observation of sensitive periods referred to in paragraph 9.3).

9.5   Time sampling is advisable since it is almost impossible to gather data of good quality from long uninterrupted periods of observation. Long stretches of fieldwork strain the capacity to describe all that is seen and heard. Furthermore, for most ethnographers the ratio of time spent writing field notes to the time spent in the field is very high. Therefore periods of observation interspersed with periods of recording and reflection are ideal and most of us have to wean ourselves of the desire to observe and record everything that goes on.

People

9.6   Social settings are never socially homogeneous: large organizations are characterized by well-defined categories and strata of personnel; more informal associations are also marked by patterns of role differentiation ('the joker', 'the butt') and such informal differentiation also occurs within formal organizations ('the office wolf'). The researcher assumes that the perspective gleaned from a given member will depend on that person's own position. A careful sampling of relevant categories of actor is therefore a necessary part of systematic fieldwork.

9.7   Members may be sampled according to their own categories – *member-identified categories*. Many ethnographic studies reveal detailed 'folk systems' of classification which reflect the abiding preoccupations of the actors themselves. For example, in a study of women prisoners Giallombardo (1966) documented the following collection of terms that the prisoners used to label fellow inmates on the basis of 'the mode of response exhibited by the inmate to the prison situation and quality of the inmate's interaction with other inmates and staff': Snitchers, Inmate Cops, Lieutenants; Squares, Jive Bitches; Rap buddies, Homeys; Connects, Boosters; Pinners; Penitentiary Turnouts, Lesbians, Femmes, Stud Broads, Tricks, Commissary Hustlers, Chippies, Kick Partners, Cherries, Punks, Turnabouts (Giallombardo, 1966, pp. 275–85). It is not possible to go into detail as to the meaning of these terms here, as it would require a fairly thorough account of everday life in the prison; and this is precisely the point: a thorough understanding of everyday life and of such 'folk' classifications are mutually dependent.

member-identified
category

9.8   People may also be sampled on the basis of *observer-identified categories*. For instance, in a study of how people behave while they are waiting, Lofland (1966) identified a number of key types: 'the sweet young things', 'the nester', 'the investigator', 'the seasoned urbanite', 'the home maverick'. In contrast to member identifications, the people so described would not recognize themselves in these terms. Such observer-identified types may be made the basis for sampling once they have been identified by the ethnographer. Thus instead of, or in addition to,

observer-identified
category

sampling by reference to class, sex, age and so on, the fieldworker may wish to sample by reference to novel categories, developed in accordance with emerging hypotheses and concepts.

SAQ 8
Spend a few minutes thinking about a setting with which you are familiar to see if you can identify different categories of actor. Think, for example, of OU tutorials or drivers on the road.

Events

9.9   Most, if not all, groups or organizations have particular occasions, gatherings, meetings and so on. They will also distinguish between activities and happenings which are routine and those which are remarkable. It is difficult to plan systematically for unusual events, but the range of normal and recurrent events should normally be sampled methodically (cf. paragraphs 9.3 to 9.5).

9.10   *Summary*   In practice, work in concrete settings will involve some sampling of time, people, and events. The three dimensions do not generate a rigid *sampling frame*, but careful attention to them can provide a basis for the controlled and systematic collection of data. In ethnographic research there is no simple way to decide on the size of any sample. In the first instance sampling is done in order to generate potentially relevant categories for data collection. Investigations will then continue until such categories have been fully explored and documented. Ideally this process would be complete when no new negative instances or novel categories were encountered, although the variety and complexity of ethnographic data and the limits of time and resources mean that in practice the ideal can only be approximated.

sampling frame

10   Combinations of Methods

10.1   It was remarked earlier in this Part (paragraph 1.13) that ethnographic research often draws upon a repertoire of different methods. The systematic use of different methods is referred to as *triangulation* (Webb *et al*, 1966). The justification for triangulation has been presented along these lines: 'Every data gathering class – interviews, questionnaires, observation, performance records, physical evidence – is potentially *biased* and has specific to it certain *validity threats*. Ideally, we should like to converge data from several different data classes, as well as converge with multiple variants within a single class' (my emphasis).

triangulation

bias,
validity threat

Interviews

10.2   Many fieldworkers complement data from participant observation with information taken from interviews. In the course of an interview the researcher can, amongst other things, investigate in more detail informants' typifications of persons and events ('Is he usually like that . . . ?' 'Would you say that was typical . . . ?' 'Could you give me an outline of a typical . . . ?'). Informants may be asked to reflect and comment upon events that have already been observed directly by the ethnographer. In addition, though, they may be used to gain information about events which occurred in this setting before the ethnographer arrived and events within the setting to which he does not have access. 'Informal' interviewing is often a part of ethnographic fieldwork. Such interviews, which are conversational in style rather than based on a fixed schedule of questions, are natural extensions of the social relationships established in the course of participant observation. More formal interviews are also sometimes used by ethnographers.

Unobtrusive Measures

10.3   Unlike most methods of social research, *unobtrusive measures* are non-reactive – that is, they avoid the problems posed by the effect of the method or the researcher on the subjects or informants (*reactivity*) – though such information is hard to check without rendering the measures reactive and obtrusive. Such measures may well be built into the design and conduct of ethnography. The researcher improvises and looks for potential indicators of relevant social processes. For instance, Sawyer (1961) counted liquor bottles in dustbins in order to estimate levels of alcohol consumption. Similarly, Phillips (1962) used a number of unobtrusive measures to estimate the effect of Cuban immigrants on Miami. He monitored, among other things, the appearance of bilingual street signs, the presence of Latin-American food on restaurant menus and the appearance of Cuban foodstuffs in supermarkets (cited by Webb *et al*, 1966, p. 119). 'Traces' such as these are given off quite naturally, and the information provided unselfconsciously.

unobtrusive measure

reactivity

Documentary Sources

10.4   These may be usefully thought of as a form of 'unobtrusive' data collection. As well as providing initial problems and questions for the research, the examination of documents provides a constant source of data during the conduct of field research (see Block 2, on the use of secondary sources in the formulation of research ideas). Where available, documentary evidence can be drawn on in order to provide systematic comparisons which can be used to develop the emerging theory.

Block 2, Parts 1 and 2

Survey Techniques

10.5   Some fieldworkers employ survey techniques in the course of ethnographic projects, to gather background data on populations or samples under investigation, or to try to assess the generality of observations made in a limited range of situations. Such an approach assumes that a survey can be used to 'check' the *representativeness* of the ethnographic data, and hence the generalizability of the interpretations. Accounts of between-method triangulation (presented in more detail in Part 6) suggest that the methods should be seen as complementary, the strengths of one remedying the weaknesses of another (e.g. a trade-off of reliability against validity). But one should be very cautious in accepting this argument. The different methods involved rely on different assumptions. For example, the participant observer will tend to stress that actors' accounts depend on the context in which they are produced, whereas the survey relies on the collection of accounts in a context that is different from everyday life and assumes the comparability of responses across interviews. We should not assume, therefore, that contrasting methods can be combined in a simple additive way.

11   Conclusion

As we have argued, the conduct of ethnography, and indeed of all research, demands a high degree of self-awareness on the part of the researcher(s). It is not possible to separate *how* the research is conducted from the 'findings', as if the 'data' existed independently of the methods used to generate them. We have outlined some of the principles according to which such research is conducted in a methodical way, so that the research procedures can be monitored and recorded in a systematic and explicit manner. An excellent example of this recording of research procedures by W. F. Whyte, has already been referred to and recommended; another has recently been published by Lacey, based on his study of a boys' Grammar school (Lacey, 1970, 1976).

SAQ 9

As a way of revising and exemplifying the ideas presented in this unit, you should now read the set article by Colin Lacey, 'Problems of sociological fieldwork: a review of the methodology of *Hightown Grammar* (reprinted in the Research in Action Reader, Ch. 8). As you read it you may find it useful to consider the following questions:

Now read Lacey (1976)

(a)   With what theoretical and methodological preconceptions was the study undertaken?

(b)   What was the original problem posed for the research?

(c)   Why was participant observation thought to be an appropriate method?

(d)   On what criteria was the setting of the research chosen?

(e)   What strategies of entry and sampling were intended, and what strategies were actually implemented?

(f)   What role(s) were adopted for the purpose of the research and to what kinds of dilemmas did these give rise?

(g)   What range of methods were used in the course of the study?

Objectives

After reading this Part you should be able to:

1   List and describe the distinctive theoretical and methodological commitments in ethnography (section 1).

2   Describe and illustrate the meaning of *progressive focusing* (section 2).

3   Distinguish between *topical* and *generic* problems (paragraphs 2.5, 2.6, 2.9, 2.10).

4   Describe the use and justification of the *comparative method* and *theoretical sampling* (paragraphs 2.7–2.13).

5   Define the meaning and use of *analytic induction* (paragraph 2.11).

6   Describe the advantages and limitations of conducting fieldwork in a familiar setting (section 5).

7   Indicate the considerations involved in the selection of a research setting, the point and time of entry (sections 3, 4 and 7).

8   Describe the interests and potential influence of *gatekeepers* in the initial stages of the research (section 6).

9 List and define the four 'master roles' adopted for fieldwork, and describe why the conscious development of field roles is an integral part of research design, data collection, evaluation and interpretation (section 8).

10 Specify principles for sampling time, people and events in the field (section 9).

Appendix

Reproduced below is a letter (from Schatzman and Strauss, 1973) sent out in the course of negotiation with gatekeepers in preparation for a study:

Dear Dr._____:
You will recall we chatted briefly at the meeting of the _____ I indicated, then, my interest in a study of changes in psychiatric organization and operations as the county system evolves from that of a centralized, professionally controlled enterprise to that of a dispersed community enterprise. I would want to discover the kinds of structural problems that may develop in this transition and, particularly, the ways these problems are defined and managed. Naturally, I hope that you will find such a study to be both interesting to you and advantageous as you and your staff ponder and deal with some of the very same problems.

In so brief a note, it is not possible to provide greater detail on the study objectives, although I would be most pleased to discuss these further with you. Here, however, I wish to assure you that I have no hidden agenda, for example, such as an effort to evaluate the work of your group; also to assure you that any future publication which may result from this study will fully generalize findings and mask the identities of persons and organization for everyone's protection.

With your permission – and that of your co-professionals – I would spend a few months observing and listening for matters related to the transition. This means making it possible for me to gain access to staff meetings and other activities which might shed some light on specific events – access at my own discretion, although not without due regard to personal (staff or patient) and clinical requirements for privacy. Except for brief interviews (really conversations) I will not 'make work' or otherwise complicate the efforts of your staff.

At later stages in the study, I will surely find one or another occasion to talk with the staff about some of my developing ideas; and surely at the conclusion of the study, I would be prepared to report to all the staff on findings pertinent to its interests. In this way, I hope my work would be of some value, and reciprocate your co-operation in the research project.

I will be phoning you within a few days, and would be happy to visit with you at any time thereafter for any matters you may wish to discuss with me.

Sincerely,

Answers to Self-assessment Questions

SAQ 1
Here are my notes. One must:

(a) identify the social meanings involved in any process of social interaction. This requires learning the culture of participants, which may take a long time and will probably require some kind of participation in the setting.

(b)   observe settings over extended periods of time in order to be able to document the processes occurring there.

(c)   carry out the research in 'natural' settings and try to adopt a role there which has minimal impact on the social interaction occurring.

(d)   try to investigate the whole organization or community, or at least settings within these rather than simply tapping the comments of single individuals.

(e)   beware of taking what people say they do on trust; try also to observe what they actually do.

SAQ 2

Social contexts in a department store:

(a)   *'Front of shop' counters*: predominantly female staff; careful self-presentation (dress, make-up); staff highly visible; customers predominantly female; low mobility and rates of interaction between staff members (from different counters and departments).

(b)   *Household basement*: staff predominantly male; less emphasis on staff self-presentation; many more male customers; staff less directly visible to customers and senior staff; higher rates of mobility and interaction between staff.

(c)   *Stores and despatch department*: staff entirely male; socially invisible; highly mobile; no concern with self-presentation; no customers.

These by no means exhaust the different locales in the shop, but perhaps give some idea of the range of social contexts that may be explored in such a setting. The differences outlined would (probably) imply different experiences of work in the shop departments, and in the nature of social interaction between the shopworkers and customers, if any.

SAQ 3

(i)   *Behaviour of pedestrians*: open access to the streets, possible difficulties in 'loitering', being 'moved on' and suspicion from passers-by.

(ii)   *Subway behaviour*: as with street behaviour, legitimate access open; similar possible troubles with loitering and observing (especially if it is obvious that observation is being made, notes taken, etc.); possible dangers as authors are all female (did you notice that?).

(iii)   *Bar sociability*: immediate access no problem; sustaining presence may prove difficult for a single person (especially a woman); may prove necessary to account for oneself and enter into negotiations from time to time; may be useful to have a 'camouflage' confederate.

(iv)   *Social structure of the restaurant*: prolonged presence and interaction with staff members requires explicit negotiations of access (e.g. in order to observe 'backstage' in the kitchen) *or* temporary employment in a number of restaurants (which may hamper research in 'front-of-house' regions).

SAQ 4

The suggested improvements by Dean *et al* (1967) are:

(a)   We want to learn how a union carries on its day-to-day work.

(b)   We want to understand how a local political party goes about a campaign.

(c)   We are interested in the different groups that make up a city like this – the Jewish community, the foreign-extraction groups – how they are organized and participate in the total life of the community.

The point about these re-phrased explanations is that they should more readily make sense to the people whose co-operation is sought (e.g. union leaders, local political leaders), and they should not appear to be threatening or critical. Of course, such gatekeepers would not be satisfied by these explanations alone. The researcher would usually be called upon to offer further, more detailed, explanations and assurances. The principle would still apply.

SAQ 5

Take the example of the Open University. A gatekeeper might wish to play up the fact that the OU model is being adopted in many parts of the world, but play down some probable reasons for this – its cheapness and the fact that it is congenial to state control over higher education. He might also play up the fact that OU courses are widely regarded as being of a very high academic standard but play down the relative failure of the OU to attract working class students as was originally intended, and play down the problems of distance teaching, etc.

SAQ 6

The precise form of negotiation would differ from one school to another and from study to study. But all or some of the following would have a legitimate interest and might well be involved:

(a) *Local authority employees*: Director or Assistant Director of Education; Chief Adviser and specialist advisers.

(b) *Members of the school*: Headteachers; Heads of Departments; individual teachers (especially if access to classrooms is requested); governors or managers.

(c) *The parents* may also be approached, particularly if individual pupils are to be singled out for intensive study.

SAQ 7

Besides the main production line there are probably a number of specialized workshops; it might be interesting for example to look at the relations between toolroom workers and men on the line since pay differentials between these groups have recently been a cause of industrial action. There are also likely to be different managerial departments, of course, such as production, sales, personnel. The Managing Director's office would probably be a key social locale though gaining access might be a problem. Shop stewards' organizations and local and national union branches might also be important settings. Notice that point of entry shapes what data is available not just in the sense that being in one setting means simultaneously not being in another, but also because one is likely to be identified with one's point of entry by members of the organization.

SAQ 8

Taking the example of drivers on the road, certain member-identified categories come to mind such as 'Sunday driver', 'cowboy', 'kerb crawler', 'speed merchant', 'road hog', 'queue jumper', 'traffic light dodger', etc. More general terms of abuse would also be relevant. One would expect specifically road relevant categories to be most developed among those categories of people who spend much of their lives behind the wheel: truck drivers, bus drivers, commercial travellers, etc. If you know anyone in this line of work you might like to ask them about this.

SAQ 9

Here, in note form, are my answers to the questions posed:

(a) *Theoretical and methodological preconceptions*:

(i)   general concern with problems of society, particularly inequality

(ii) anthropology and sociology: blend of functionalism and conflict theory

(iii) participant observation but fairly catholic attitude to methods.

(b) *Original problem*:

(i)   under-achievement of working class pupils (note link with concern over social inequality).

(c) *Choice of participant observation*:

(i)   to get at different views and capture social processes – to explore the 'black box'; but also a concern to check the models generated because of the danger of bias.

(d) *Choice of school*:

(i) grammar school as extreme case in relation to pupil failure

(ii) typical insofar as had a stable relationship with the community.

(e) *Strategies of entry and sampling*:

(i) access from above

(ii) for first year – teacher role to gain and maintain access and trust

(iii) teaching as important source of data – sampling participant experience – in practice only taught first, second and sixth forms

(iv) initially intended to cover whole school from lower school to sixth form by studying three differently located groups of pupils longitudinally for three years; in fact by the second term had to give up following one of these groups

(v) in final stages move out of the school into the community; never did do this because of constraints of his role as university teacher.

(f) *Roles*:

(i) initially participant observer, being a part-time teacher in the school; later more of an observing participant as far as the teacher role was concerned, but perhaps more of a participant from point of view of pupils?

(ii) two key dilemmas – standing in for a teacher taking a class, some of whose members he had already established informal relations with – conflict between teacher and researcher roles

(iii) whether to pass on confidential information where it might help a pupil – conflict between researcher role and human values.

(g) *Research methods:*

(i) participation

(ii) observation

(iii) informal interviews with teachers and pupils; special discussion groups with the latter

(iv) quasi-experiment of a primitive kind (did you notice that?)

(v) documents

(vi) questionnaires.

References

ATKINSON, P. A. (1976) *The clinical experience: an ethnography of medical education*, unpublished PhD thesis, University of Edinburgh.

BALL, D. (1972) 'Self and identity in the context of deviance: the case of criminal abortion', in Scott, R. A. and Douglas, J. D. (eds) (1972) *Theoretical perspectives on deviance*, New York, Basic Books. Reprinted in Wilson, M. J. (ed.) (1979) Ch. 9.

BECKER, H. S. and GEER, B. (1958) 'The fate of idealism in medical school', *American Sociological Review*, Vol. 23, February, pp. 50–6. Reprinted in Wilson, M. J. (ed.) (1979) Ch. 15.

BECKER, H. S., GEER, B., HUGHES, E. C. and STRAUSS, A. L. (1961) *Boys in white: student culture in medical school*, Chicago, University of Chicago Press.

BERNSTEIN, B. and DAVIES, B. (1969) 'Some sociological comments on Plowden', in Peters, R. S. (ed.) (1972) *Perspectives on Plowden*, London, Routledge and Kegan Paul. Reprinted in Wilson, M. J. (ed.) (1979) Ch. 4.

BIRENBAUM, A. and SAGARIN, E. (eds) (1973) *People and places: the sociology of the familiar*, London, Nelson.

BOGDAN, J. and TAYLOR, S. J. (1973) *Introduction to qualitative research methods*, New York, John Wiley and Sons.

BYNNER, J. and STRIBLEY, K. M. (eds) (1979) *Social research: principles and procedures*, London, Longman/The Open University Press (Course Reader).

CAVAN, S. (1973) 'Bar sociability', in Birenbaum, A. and Sagarin, E. (eds) (1973) Pt. III, Ch. 1, pp. 143–54.

DEAN, J. P., EICHHORN, R. L. and DEAN, L. R. (1967) 'Establishing field relations', in McCall, G. J. and Simmons, J. L. (eds) *Issues in participant observation*, Reading, Mass., Addison-Wesley.

DENZIN, N. K. (1970) *The research act in sociology*, London, Butterworths.

DEUTSCHER, I. (1966) 'Words and deeds: social science and social policy', *Social Problems*, Vol. 13, pp. 233–54.

GEER, B. (1964) 'First days in the field' in Hammond, P. (ed.) *Sociologists at work*, New York, Basic Books.

GIALLOMBARDO, R. (1966) 'Social roles in a prison for women', *Social Problems*, Vol. 13, pp. 268–88.

GLASER, B. and STRAUSS, A. L. (1967) *The discovery of grounded theory*, Chicago, Aldine.

GOFFMAN, E. (1968) *Asylums*, Harmondsworth, Penguin.

GOFFMAN, E. (1971) *The presentation of self in everyday life*, Harmondsworth, Penguin.

GOLD, R. L. (1958) 'Roles in sociological field observations', *Social Forces*, Vol. 36, pp. 217–23.

GOODY, J. (1976) *Production and reproduction*, Cambridge, Cambridge University Press.

HAMILTON, D. (1976) *Curriculum evaluation*, London, Open Books.

HARGREAVES, D. (1967) *Social relations in a secondary school*, London, Routledge and Kegan Paul.

JUNKER, B. (1960) *Fieldwork*, Chicago, University of Chicago Press.

KELLY, G. (1955) *The psychology of personal constructs* (2 vols) New York, Norton.

LACEY, C. (1970) *Hightown Grammar*, Manchester, University of Manchester Press.

LACEY, C. (1976) 'Problems of sociological fieldwork: a review of the methodology of *Hightown Grammar*', in Shipman, M. (ed.) *The organization and impact of social research*, London, Routledge and Kegan Paul. Reprinted in Wilson, M. J. (ed.) (1979) Ch. 8. (Set Reading.)

LEVINE, J., VINSON, A. and WOOD, D. (1969) 'Subway behaviour', in Birenbaum, A. and Sagarin, E. (eds) (1973) Pt. IV, Ch. 2, pp. 208–16.

LINDESMITH, A. R. (1947) *Opiate addiction*, Bloomington, Ind., Principia Press.

LINDESMITH, A. R. (1968) *Addiction and opiates*, Chicago, Aldine.

LOFLAND, L. (1966) 'In the presence of strangers: a study of behaviour in public settings', Working Paper No. 19 of The Center for Research on Social Organization, University of Michigan.

LOFLAND, J. (1971) *Analyzing social settings*, Belmont, Cal., Wadsworth.

LOFLAND, J. (1977) *Doing social life*, New York, John Wiley and Sons.

MacDONALD, B. and WALKER, R. (1976) *Changing the curriculum*, London, Open Books.

PHILLIPS, R. H. (1962) 'Miami goes Latin under Cuban tide', *The New York Times,* March 18, cited by Webb *et al* (1966).

PLOWDEN REPORT (1967) *Children and their primary schools*, Central Advisory Council for Education (England), Vol. 1: Report, Vol. 2: Research and surveys, London, HMSO.

SAWYER, H. G. (1961) 'The meaning of numbers', speech to American Association of Advertising Agencies, cited by Webb *et al* (1966).

SCHATZMAN, L. and STRAUSS, A. L. (1973) *Field research*, Englewood Cliffs, Prentice-Hall.

SHIPMAN, M., BOLAM, D. and JENKINS, D. (1974) *Inside a curriculum project: a case study in the process of curriculum change*, London, Methuen.

SHOTTER, J. (1975) *Images of man in psychological research*, London, Methuen.

STRAUSS, A. L., SCHATZMAN, L., EHRLICH, D., BUCHER, R. and SABSHIN, M. (1963) 'The hospital and its negotiated order', in Freidson (ed.) *The hospital in modern society*, Glencoe, Ill., Free Press.

STUBBS, M. and DELAMONT, S. (eds) (1976) *Explorations in classroom observation*, London, John Wiley and Sons.

WEBB, E. (1966) 'Unconventionality, triangulation and inference', in proceedings of the *1966 Invitational conference on testing problems*, Princeton, Educational Testing Service.

WEBB, E. J., CAMPBELL, D. T., SCHWARTZ, R. D. and SECHREST, L. (1966) *Unobtrusive measures: nonreactive research in the social sciences*, Chicago, Rand McNally.

WHYTE, W. F. (1955) 'Methodological appendix', in *Street corner society*, Chicago, University of Chicago Press. (Abridged version supplied as Supplementary Material; Set Reading.)

WHYTE, W. F. (1973) 'The social structure of the restaurant', in Birenbaum, A. and Sagarin, E. (eds) Pt. V, Ch. 1, pp. 244–56.

WILSON, M. J. (ed.) (1979) *Social and educational research in action: a book of readings*, London, Longman/The Open University Press (Course Reader).

WISEMAN, J. P. (1974) 'The research web', *Urban life and culture*, Vol. 3, No. 3, pp. 317–28. Reprinted in Bynner, J. and Stribley, K. M. (eds) (1979) Ch. 10.

WOLFF, M. (1973) 'Notes on the behavior of pedestrians', in Birenbaum, A. and Sagarin, E. (eds) (1973) Pt. I, Ch. 2, pp. 35–48.

WOODS, P. and HAMMERSLEY, M. (eds) (1977) *School experience*, London, Croom Helm.

Part 6   Evaluation of Research Designs
Prepared by Jeff Evans for the Course Team

Block 3 Part 6

Contents

Introduction

'Since each style has different emphases, and consequently different strengths and weaknesses, the careful researcher should try to combine the styles in a way that is appropriate to the problem being investigated.'

'The three styles represent the methodological aspects of very different traditions in social theory and social research; it is therefore illusory to think that they can be combined in any simple way.'

These are examples of the sorts of apparently conflicting positions that were put forward in the Course Team as we discussed the three styles and their appropriateness for particular research problems. The earlier Parts of the course have given you some insight into the range of problems investigated by researchers in the three styles and the range of methods used. In this Part, I focus on comparisons between the styles and on the possibilities of combining them.

Aims

1   To summarize the decisions made at the design stage of research in the three styles (as discussed earlier in the Block), the criteria by which these decisions are made, and the methods used to carry them out.

2   To illustrate the possibility of combining elements from all three styles through a discussion of a research project which aimed to evaluate the effectiveness of a particular teaching innovation.

Study Guide

Work systematically through the text, completing the reading and attempting the SAQs and questions at the points indicated. The extract from Kish (1959) should be read for the exercise in section 1. Since there are frequent references back to Parts 1, 2 and 3 of the Block, it is best to have these available. The questions available on 'Cicero' (the computer-based tutorial system) will provide useful revision for this Part and for the whole Block.

Set Reading

KISH, L. (1959) 'Some statistical problems in research design', in Bynner, J. and Stribley, K. M. (eds) (1979) *Social research: principles and procedures*, Ch. 8.

Recommended Reading

SJOBERG, G. and NETT, R. (1968) *Methodology for social research*, pp. 92–5, 108–12 and 117–20.

SMITH, H. W. (1975) *Strategies of social research: the methodological imagination*, Ch. 1. (Set Book.)

Further Reading

The following books and articles may interest you if you would like to read more about the topics discussed in this Part.

On experiments and quasi-experiments in the field:

CAMPBELL, D. T. and STANLEY, J. C. (1963) 'Experimental and quasi-experimental designs for research on teaching', in Gage, N. L. (ed.) (1963) *Handbook of research on teaching*, Ch. 5, Chicago, Rand McNally; reprinted as a booklet (1966).

On the possibility of links between experimental and ethnographic research at the theoretical level:

HARRE, R. and SECORD, P. F. (1971) *The explanation of social behaviour*, Oxford, Basil Blackwell.

On the links between the ethnographic and other styles of research at the philosophical level:

GIDDENS, A. (1976) *New rules of sociological method*, London, Hutchinson.

Experimental (Block 3, Part 2, paragraph 7.1)	**Survey** (Block 3, Part 3, paragraph 6.5)	**Ethnographic** (Block 3, Part 5)
	Assessment of resources and constraints (a)	
Formulation of problem (a)	Structuring the problem, including clarification of hypotheses and specifying controls (b)	Formulation of problems (topical and generic) (paragraph 2.5)
Articulation of hypothesis (b)		
Use of sources (b)		
Devising controls for internal validity (d)		
Choice of setting(s) (e)		Choosing and constituting the setting (sections 3–5)
	Specifying population and sample (c)	
	Deciding on method of data collection (postal questionnaires, interviews, etc.) (d)	
Specifying indicators for dependent and independent variables, and preparing measuring instruments, if necessary (c)	Designing the questionnaire or interview schedule (e)	
	Piloting and revision of hypotheses, schedules, measurement/scaling procedures (f)	Casing the setting (section 3)
	Negotiating access to respondents in some surveys (Block 3, Part 4, paragraphs 2.6–2.12)	Negotiation of access ('getting in', section 6)
		Choosing the time and place of entry (section 7)
		Mapping (section 7)
		Establishment of field role (section 8)
Carrying out laboratory (or field) experiment	Fieldwork (g)	(Constant) sampling of people, events and time (section 9)
		Combining methods ('triangulation') (section 10)
		Combining methods hypotheses via the comparative method and theoretical sampling (section 2)
Analysis	Data processing and analysis (h)	Analysis
Report of results	Report writing (i)	Final report
Replication, especially in field settings (e and f)		

1 Decisions in Research Design

1.1 Throughout the Block we have discussed a variety of decisions that are made at the design stage of a research project. At this point it seems useful to prepare at least a provisional summary of the sorts of decisions involved across the three styles. Later in this section, I shall discuss the various commitments and constraints that affect social research and illustrate the way they affect design decisions.

1.2 Using what I found in earlier Parts of the Block on 'stages of research', I compiled the list given in Table 1, attempting to keep the decision points in roughly the same order for all three styles.

1.3 Clearly this list depends to some extent on the particular account of each style given in the sections referred to. On reflection, we find that similarities among the styles, in terms of the decisions that must be taken, are even greater than the list suggests. For example, we know that research in all three styles is subject to resource and other constraints; in each style, too, the researcher consults existing sources before collecting new data (Block 2). Piloting is useful not only in the survey style, but in the experimental (e.g. to test instrumentation) and in the ethnographic (e.g. in 'casing the setting'). And at the design stage in all three styles, we have to look ahead to the preparation of data, its analysis and its interpretation.

Does Table 1 suggest any great differences in the styles?

Table 1 (left) List of stages in research in the three styles

1.4   The main difference between the styles suggested by the list has to do with the use of hypotheses. Each style must be concerned with hypotheses, since these are the 'guiding ideas' of the research; in particular, they determine what data should be *selected* as relevant to the research. The experimenter clearly sets out his/her hypothesis – or several hypotheses – *in advance* of the research. For explanatory surveys, the same can be done – and this will be extremely helpful (indispensable) in drawing up the questionnaire or interview schedule – but both hypotheses and schedule will probably undergo revision and further articulation after the piloting stage. Finally, the ethnographic style has the most fluid manner of progressively focusing hypotheses during the fieldwork *and* analysis stages.

1.5   The other important difference has to do with the establishment of field roles. Any researcher, of course, has to adopt a role in interacting with various participants in the study. But the styles differ in terms of the range of roles adopted by the researcher and, correspondingly, in the roles attributed to participants. In surveys, the interviewer typically claims to be adopting a 'neutral' role so as not to affect the answers given by the respondent (we shall discuss the problem of interviewer bias in Block 4, Parts 1 and 2). On the other hand, the experimenter is clearly active in allocating treatments to subjects, in controlling laboratory conditions, and sometimes in setting up temporary deception (as in the Milgram experiments). And the ethnographer chooses one of several possible roles *vis à vis* the actors in the setting being studied and attempts to describe its effect on the findings.

1.6   We shall discuss the sequence of decisions made in the course of a research project more fully in Block 8. I now want to discuss some of the criteria that guide these decisions; these have to do with various *commitments* of the researcher and the *constraints* within which the research is designed and carried out.

Commitments and Constraints

1.7   Throughout this Block, we have considered three 'tensions' between theory and data and associated methodological problems (Block 3, Part 1, paragraphs 1.9–1.13 and Figure 2). These are as follows:

(i)   *Construct v. indicator*   problems of measurement and description

(ii)   *Causation v. correlation*   problems of control and explanation

(iii) *Population v. sample*   problems of representation and generalization

1.8   Of course, there is no such thing as a perfect study: 'In practice, we cannot solve simultaneously all the problems of measurement, representation, and control; rather one must choose and compromise' (Kish, 1959, p. 397). For many of the problems we are discussing there are no absolutely right or wrong solutions. The research process can be seen as series of *trade-offs*: most of the decisions you take are such that you get more of one desired outcome at the cost of having less of another. Therefore, the problem is much more complex than simply avoiding a set of errors or biases that anyone with a good memory could list. In evaluating or designing a piece of research, we may often want to ascertain what is gained and what is lost by a certain choice.

trade-off

1.9   Sometimes, the researcher chooses a particular method or technique by comparing its strengths or weaknesses for a specific research problem with those of the available alternatives. Sometimes, however, researchers make choices based on their commitments, for example on the *methodological commitments* inherent in the style within which (s)he is working. At this point in the course, we can begin to compare the three styles of research in terms of the amount of emphasis placed on the problems raised by each of the three tensions and the methods used to deal with these problems.

methodological commitment

"TRADE-OFFS"

1.10 An example of the sorts of trade-off we can expect has to do with the criteria of internal and external validity (Block 3, Part 1, section 4) for evaluating a given study. We have generally found that a study designed to be strong on internal validity tends to be weak on population validity or on ecological validity or both. (Further illustrations of trade-offs will be discussed in paragraphs 1.24–1.30.) The next paragraph discusses, in broad terms, the relationship between, on the one hand, the methodological problems associated with the three tensions, and on the other, internal and external (population and ecological) validity.

1.11 (a) We might say, first of all, that the *internal validity* of an *explanation* of the findings of a given study depends on the effectiveness of the *controls* (of alternative explanatory hypotheses) used.

(b) Similarly, the *external validity* of any *generalization* of the findings (to some population of interest) depends on the *representativeness* of the sampling. However, we may attempt to generalize not only from a sample to a population of individuals – in which case we are concerned with *population* validity; but also to other settings (times and places) or to other events – in which case, our concern would be *ecological* validity (Block 3, Part 1, paragraphs 4.17 and 4.18).

(c) It is clearly impossible for the sample of individuals, settings and events studied in a particular project to be representative for the purpose of all conceivable generalizations that a given researcher and the readers of his or her reports might wish to consider. Therefore the external validity of a generalization must rest not only on the technical merits of the sampling procedure used but also on the adequacy of the *description* of the setting of the research and the relevant events. For our purpose 'events' can be considered to include the administering of various versions of the treatment (Campbell, 1969, p. 411) and the taking of measurements of 'explanatory variables' (Kish, 1959). External validity can thus be seen to be related to the construct *v*. indicator tension. Ethnographic description is clearly likely to be important here, and we shall see in section 2 that it can also be used to strengthen internal validity. (The problem of the validity of *measurement* will be discussed in Blocks 4 and 5.)

Activity

For each of the styles, consider the following 'ideal-type' design:

Experimental: random assignment of individuals to comparison groups; treatments allocated by the experimenter; behavioural indicators in laboratory conditions.

Survey: standardized verbal responses to a questionnaire 'administered' to a probability sample in the 'field' by an interviewer.

Ethnographic: 'participant-observation' study of the process of social life in a natural setting, with particular attention to understanding individual and group 'meanings'.

For each of the three styles, indicate:

(a) the relative emphasis placed on control, representation and description;

(b) the methods of control used;

(c) the methods of representation used; and

(d) the relative strength of the concern with internal and external validity.

Note that at this stage of the course I am asking you merely to sketch the methodological commitments of each style and not to make definitive comparisons or evaluations of the styles. (We shall compare the three styles more fully in Block 8.)

There are a number of resources you can use for this exercise. First of all, review the sections in this Block on commitments and 'strengths' and 'weaknesses', of each of the three styles: experimental (Part 2, section 6), survey (Part 3, section 1) and ethnographic (Part 5, section 1).

Second, read the set extract from Kish (1959) 'Some statistical problems in research design', Ch. 8 in the Principles and Procedures Reader. Read only the section headed 'Experiments, surveys, and other investigations'. Kish makes a number of instructive points about the styles of research, especially experiments and surveys; note that Kish's 'investigations' are not necessarily ethnographic: if 'controlled' they may be quasi-experiments (see Part 2).

Read Kish (1959)

Third, remembering the accounts you have read of the research in the various styles should also help; for example, you could compare the description of the research setting given in the accounts of Milgram's experiments (the laboratory), the Plowden survey (the parent's home or the child's classroom), and Whyte's ethnography (various everyday locales in Cornerville). Use the chart below to summarize your comparison of the styles. Spend no more than 20 minutes reviewing the earlier sections, 20 minutes skimming Kish and 20 minutes completing the chart; do not worry if you have to leave some blanks.

Aspect	Experimental	Survey	Ethnographic
(a) Relative emphasis (with each style) on control, representation and description	Control v. strong also rep.	Rep strong controls less so Also desc.	Descriph. strong. less + rep. less on control.
(b) Methods of control	Random allocatin to treatment groups. Standardized test conditions	Statistical controls - time series, repeated contact	Comparative method Theoretical sampling inductive method
(c) Methods of representation	Sometim prob sampling - not as good as should	Statistical - prob sampling perhaps cluster	Theoretical + methodical sampling
(d) Relative concern with internal and external validity	Strong o internal less o external.	Half o half o bot	Not strong ecological poss i ecological val - emphasis o naturalism

When you have completed your notes for this exercise you might like to compare them with mine given in the Appendix.

_____

1.12 The focus of this exercise was on the *methodological commitments* involved in the three styles. These include different emphases on the problems related to the three tensions, different methods used to resolve these problems and different concerns with internal and external validity.

1.13 We might also mention the *conceptual commitments*, inherent in any research, to a certain theoretical system used to describe and to explain the world. We have seen that this helps to shape the selection of problems as theoretically worthy of research (Block 2, Part 1) and to determine which explanations are plausible (Block 3, Part 1). One example which differentiates among the styles would be the commitment to explanation-by-understanding (i.e. in terms of the actor's ideas), which is much stronger in ethnography though by no means lacking in all surveys or experiments. On the other hand, as we shall see, it is common for researchers sharing a set of conceptual commitments to use more than one style of research.

conceptual commitment

1.14 In addition, we must consider the *political and social commitments* of the researcher, the research community and society, as well as, where relevant, those of the organization which has commissioned the research; examples of organizations which do so are the State (e.g. the Department of Education and Science) and commercial organizations (for market research and opinion polling). These commitments help to shape the selection of research projects as practically relevant and determine whether or not a given explanation is 'practical' (Block 3, Part 1). They also bring with them assumptions about which aspects of society, or of a given organization, should be maintained and which changed (Smith, 1975, p.3). In addition they affect the use made of the results of research; for example, to whom are they available and at what cost? (We shall discuss political commitments further in Block 8.)

political and social commitments

1.15 Closely related to political commitments are *ethical commitments*. Indeed, we could say that the former have to do with preferred *ends*, and the latter with *means* (or ways of treating people) that are considered correct – or at least preferable – by the researcher, the research community and society.

ethical commitment

One method of dealing with the methodological problem of control involves the allocation of different treatments by the experimenter. Give an example of a case where such allocation would raise ethical problems. (Some examples are given in Smith, 1975, Ch. 1.) Can you think of any other examples of ethical problems relevant to the design stage of research?

Milgram's exp.

Education research new
teaching eg – should.
Some children miss out?

1.16 First of all, ethical difficulties rule out the allocation of (potentially) harmful treatments (e.g. the smoking of cigarettes) to some members of the research sample. They may also arise in depriving some people of a potentially beneficial treatment, for example, a *new* teaching method which can only be allocated to the experimental group while the control group is allocated the traditional method. In comparison with some experimental treatments, the intrusion into people's *privacy* by a survey conducted in the home or on the street corner, or by the presence of an ethnographer in one's everyday situation, may seem slight. However, for potentially sensitive areas, such as sexual behaviour, interviews and participant observation might well be considered intrusive; questionnaires would be less so.

1.17 There may also be ethical dilemmas in the way that participants are *recruited* to a certain study. In experiments, this has often involved the use of compulsion or remuneration; for example, many experiments have used under-graduate subjects who were required to participate in the experiment as part of their course-work. Neither type of motivation seems necessary to get most respondents to talk to most survey researchers; none-the-less each householder in Britain is legally compelled to fill in a Census form. In most surveys, however, respondents may choose to exercise their freedom not to talk to the researcher; the 'non response' rate may give an indication of how many have done so. In ethnography, it seems that respondents can choose not to talk to researchers, just by avoiding them, or can use various defences such as deception against them even while apparently involved in an interview (Argyris, 1952).

1.18 A third type of ethical dilemma arises in deciding on whether to deceive participants, even if it will be only temporary. This is illustrated by the deception of subjects as to the genuineness of the shocks they were giving in Milgram's experiments, by a surveyor asking respondents about their opinion on non-existent legislation[1] and by secret ethnographic research (Block 3, Part 5, paragraph 8.2; Block 4, Part 3). Of course there is no guarantee that any particular deception will be successful (Crowle, 1976).

1.19 Some researchers react to these dilemmas by arguing for an absolute code of ethics, which would forbid any researcher to use certain practices under any circumstances; others would leave such decisions to the conscience of the individual researcher concerned (Smith, 1975, p. 5). These decisions are complex since they ultimately involve a judgement as to the practical value of the research project. In paragraphs 1.24–1.27 below I will illustrate *trade-offs* that often occur between ethical and other commitments, in making a particular research decision.

1.20 Finally, we need to consider the *resources* available for a given study; these include money, time and labour from various people, access to machines (e.g. computers) and so on. These are generally provided – or denied – by society (rather than by the researchers themselves). Also important are the time available (if the project has a deadline) and access to the groups to be studied. Any given project may or may not allow trade-offs among different sorts of resource.

1.21 The question of the amount of resources (in various forms) commanded by the researcher is related not only to his or her ability to write convincing research proposals but also to the power and status in society of the individual, and of the groups to which (s)he belongs (notably, the 'discipline' and the institution). I cannot go into the issue of the social position of the researcher in detail here, but I can recommend you to read the relevant passages from Sjoberg and Nett (1968) pp. 92–5, 108–12 and 117–20.

1.22 It is worth remembering that groups who might be studied have their own 'resources' too. First of all, powerful groups such as the cabinet and high-ranking military officers can often prevent access to their everyday settings; they do not have to volunteer for experiments and they can legitimately refuse interviews (on

[1]*When a sample of Americans were asked their opinions of the 'Metallic Metals Act' of 1947, seventy per cent gave a clear verdict of approval or disapproval (Marsh, 1979).*

the grounds of being busy, etc.). Secondly, any group or any individual can engage in their own types of deception by putting up 'fronts' (Block 4, Part 3).

1.23 To recapitulate, I have described the methodological, conceptual, political and ethical commitments, and the resource constraints that condition the decisions made throughout a research project.

1.24 I shall now discuss the role of the various types of commitments in a research decision. Sometimes this is fairly straightforward. For example, survey researchers with a methodological commitment to representation will tend to select the participants for a study using a probability sampling method from a pre-specified population. An experimenter who had less of a commitment to representation or whose conceptual system suggested that all human beings were the same in terms of the factors being investigated would tend to select the most convenient participants. That is, he will use his scarce resources, such as time, to deal with other methodological problems, such as control. This would be an example of a *trade-off* (paragraph 1.8): a saving of resources, at the cost of less attention to representation, and hence, lower external validity. Let us consider some further examples.

SAQ 1
Given the information that Milgram recruited volunteers for his first experiment through newspaper advertisements offering $4 for 'one hour of your time':

(a) What people do you think would be included in the population to which he could generalize the results of this particular experiment?

(b) What would be the effect of offering $8 while holding constant the total resources available?

SAQ 2
If you thought that less well-educated people would tend to be more obedient to a psychologist, how would you assess whether the sample was less well-educated on average, than the general population? (Assume in *this* case that the general population of interest is 'all living Americans'.)

1.25 SAQs 1a and 2 show how we can assess the external population validity of a study, by comparing the sample to the general population in terms of certain characteristics considered to be related to the variable of interest: interest in psychological research and educational level respectively were thought to be related both to the likelihood of being recruited and to obedient behaviour towards a psychologist. SAQ 1b illustrates the trade-off between two desirable characteristics of a sampling procedure. Similarly we can envisage trade-offs between ethical and other commitments.

For example, what was the trade-off in terms of gains and losses to the researchers and subjects from the use of deception in the Milgram experiments?

1.26 Through the use of deception (in allocating 'teacher' and 'learner' roles and in pretending that the dials were connected to a real shock generator), Milgram was able to present a situation that was actually created to measure the obedience of the teacher, as one concerned with the progress of the learner. He thereby cut out a major *reactive* threat to his results, viz. the subject knowing what he was studying. He would probably say that the short period during which the subject was deceived (from the beginning of the experiment until the de-briefing interview at the end) was a small price to pay for this improvement; further, 'the central moral justification for allowing a procedure of the sort used in my experiment is that it is judged acceptable by those who have taken part in it' (Milgram, 1974, p. 199).

1.27 Besides offending the *ethical* commitment of the researcher or of society, an act like deception may have *consequences* which will affect the research because it is offensive to subjects. For example, being made aware of the deception might possibly have aroused a certain resentment in some subjects, that might have made it less likely that they would respond openly during the de-briefing interview.

1.28 The fact that the illustrations of trade-offs in the preceding paragraphs are taken from experimental research should not be taken to suggest that it is only in the experimental style that trade-offs have to be made. For example, ethnographers generally work in a naturalistic setting in order to increase ecological validity, but this means that they have less opportunity to use controls and hence internal validity is a problem. Survey researchers may cut down on non-response – and improve population validity – by calling on respondents later in the evening, but badgering them too much may ultimately be considered an invasion of privacy.

1.29 Sometimes too, the researchers are constrained by what actually happens when they enter the field. For example, in the study of computer-assisted instruction (to be described in section 2), their choice of research design was severely constrained by the political commitments and interests of *other* institutions and individuals in the setting of the study.

1.30 The examples above illustrate how research decisions might be made in response to a trade-off between two methodological commitments or a trade-off between methodological and ethical commitments. Research is made up of decisions that are like this. Thus:

> the social scientist is not value-free or value-neutral in his research. The least that can be asked of him is, first, that he be aware of his value biases and know how they influence his research efforts, and second, that he try to minimize his value positions in his research. (Smith, 1975, p. 15)

2 Combinations of the Three Styles

2.1 Now that we have looked at the various commitments of the styles and some of their strengths and weaknesses, the natural question to ask is whether elements of two or more styles could be used in one research project. There seem to be few examples of this in the literature; sometimes, however, a study which appears to be simply located within one style can be seen, on closer examination, to use elements of more than one style. For example, Colin Lacey's *Hightown Grammar* (1970) used ethnographic, survey and even experimental methods (see Block 3, Part 5, SAQ 9g).

2.2   In this section I will outline, in some detail, a study with which I was involved, which aimed at the evaluation of a particular teaching method in the United States in the late 1960s, and which used elements of all three styles of research. One of the options within the formative TMA connected with this Block requires you to evaluate the design of the study under a number of headings.

The Evaluation of Computer-assisted Instruction

2.3   In the 1960s educators in the West, and especially in the United States, were struggling to 'catch up' with the Russian educational system, the superiority of which was implied by the launching of the Sputnik satellite in 1957. None-the-less, the economy was buoyant and there was great faith that money spent on educational *research* followed by *development* of innovations would bear fruit in the form of higher levels of educational achievement. This section discusses an example of the third stage in the process, that of *evaluation* of innovations.

2.4   Many of the innovations being developed in the USA consisted of various forms of technology: machines (hardware) and procedures (software) that could be developed centrally, often at great expense, and then installed in a large number of schools or systems of schools. One such new technology was 'computer-assisted instruction' (CAI) which was to be used for drill and practice in teaching in a number of subjects, notably in primary school arithmetic. CAI was based on the ideas of programmed instruction[2] but used the computer as a more flexible mode of presenting material than the programmed texts or teaching machines developed earlier.

2.5   By the mid-1960s, CAI had been tried out in a number of schools, but predominantly in those most accessible to University researchers: schools geographically or administratively linked to universities in New York City and the San Francisco area in California. Experiments had been designed with great attention to internal validity, but external validity was still in question: would CAI help pupils to learn arithmetic in ordinary schools? To answer this required *replication* of the earlier research to see if its findings could be generalized, say, to rural areas.

replication

2.6   The choice of setting for the evaluation research was influenced not only by the aim of increasing external validity, but also, as always in research, by practical questions of convenience and constraints. What was perhaps the main CAI programme in arithmetic had been developed at Stanford University, near San Francisco (Suppes *et al*, 1968). A large-scale evaluation of CAI launched somewhere else could create a sort of competition amongst the pupils in the two settings for the time of the computer where the CAI programme was located. However, since the United States covers four major time zones from east to west, pupils in the eastern time zone could use the computer all morning before students in California arrived at school. It only remained to find an organization that could manage to install CAI terminals in schools in some part of the eastern time zone, and could gain access for researchers to carry out an evaluation of the innovation. CEMREL, the St Louis 'regional laboratory' of the US Office of Education was able to undertake this, in co-operation with EKEDC, the Eastern Kentucky Educational Development Corporation, which was supported by state and local authorities.

2.7   The major aim of the CAI study was to determine the nature and size of any gains in arithmetic skills due to the use of computerized drill in the schools of the

---

[2]*Programmed instruction entails the breaking down of the material to be learned into small steps arranged carefully into an appropriate sequence; success at one step is rewarded or 'reinforced' before the student goes on to the next. Students generally work through this material individually, rather than in groups.*

area. Since it was recognized that the effect of CAI would be dependent on the way it was used, a second aim was to describe the use made of the innovation by teachers, pupils and schools, and the impact it made on them. A third aim was to describe changes in the attitudes of teachers, pupils and parents towards CAI as a result of its installation, in order to assess the possibilities for the wider diffusion of the innovation (Russell, 1969, p. 1). Pilot work and casing of the setting (see Part 5, paragraph 3.10) were carried out during the school year 1967–68, and the main study was planned for 1968–69.

2.8   In connection with the aim of assessing any gains that might be due to the use of CAI, one set of early decisions had to do with the choice of research design (Russell and Evans, 1969). Previous evaluations of CAI had been experimental; for this reason, the researchers planning the Eastern Kentucky study had a methodological commitment to using at least a component of experimentation there.

Recall our notion of an 'ideal experiment' (see Activity on p. 92). Was such a design possible in this setting?

2.9   Since we wanted to maximize the external validity of the series of CAI studies, we needed to do this study in ordinary schools, i.e. in the field rather than in a laboratory. However, it did seem possible to establish two comparable groups of students, preferably by random allocation of pupils to groups, assign CAI to one group, but not the other, and then to measure their scores for arithmetic skills of various kinds at the end of the year. (Standardized tests in arithmetic *computation*, *concepts* and *applications*, developed at Stanford University, were available.) An obvious way to do this has been called by Campbell and Stanley the 'post-test only control group' design (Smith, 1975, pp. 84–5) and can be represented by a 'design scheme' as in Figure 1.

2.10   However, we were interested in the size of *gains* over the period of using CAI for the two groups and not just in whether or not the CAI group finished up with a higher score than the non-CAI group. Thus, we decided to use the 'pre-test, post-test control group' design (Smith, 1975, pp. 83–4); a design scheme for this is shown in Figure 2.

2.11   This was fine for the structure of the design but what units (schools, classes, individual pupils) could be randomly assigned to CAI? Here we came up against political constraints in the form of interests of other institutions and groups. Could we as researchers randomly assign CAI to some *schools* in the area and not to others? No, because the CAI schools were chosen by the local organization of the EKEDC, on the basis of one per district. Could we then randomly assign *teachers* to CAI or not? No, because within each school, the head chose the teachers, often those considered to be the most favourable to innovation, for the CAI classes. This is understandable: it was presumably so as to give the innovation a good chance and to establish the head's school as one of

Figure 1   Post-test only control group design

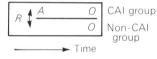

A represents the action or treatment (i.e. CAI)
O represents an observation
R indicates random allocation to the two groups

Figure 2   Pre-test, post-test control group design

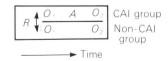

99

the more forward-looking ones in the region. (Assessment of these sorts of hypotheses clearly required an ethnographic component to the research.)

2.12   We then considered whether it was possible to *match* a non-CAI school with each CAI school chosen by the administrators (for a discussion of matching see Part 2, paragraph 3.5). This required ideas about what were the important characteristics for matching schools in a study of this kind. However, we were not sure what these characteristics were before we began the research. In addition we were not sure that we would be able, in practical terms, to find a school to match another, even if we had articulated the matching criteria. We finally decided to randomly assign pupils *within* each classroom/teacher unit to have CAI or not. This would allow us to produce a randomized design within the administrative constraints detailed above.

2.13   Here we ran up against ethical and political constraints. If we randomly assigned half the pupils in a classroom to a CAI group and the other half to a non-CAI group, the pupils would almost certainly tell their parents; and the parents might raise objections if their child were not having access to something they considered good, or conversely, if their child were being directed to use the computer terminal against their wishes. We decided to cope with this difficulty by creating two experimental periods: those pupils in CAI classes who did not receive CAI during the first semester would automatically receive it during the second semester, and vice-versa. Note that this meant that all pupils *within CAI classes* were to have equal access to CAI, and we were still able to randomly allocate pupils within these classrooms to have access to CAI or not, for each of two semesters during the year of the main study. These pupils were given pre- and post-tests in arithmetic skills, as were pupils within certain non-CAI classes, selected for comparison purposes. Thus we had a true experimental design *within* CAI classes and a quasi-experimental design (see Part 2) between CAI and non-CAI classes.

SAQ 3
Draw a 'design scheme' for the design we finally decided to use.

2.14   Because CAI was not allocated to classes at random, but rather on the basis of political factors (see paragraph 2.11), we had to consider threats to the internal validity of comparisons between CAI and non-CAI *classes* at the analysis stage.

What factors, other than the presence or absence of the treatment, do you think might have been likely to explain differences in the CAI and non-CAI classes at the analysis stage?

Maturation anyway.
Type of school allocated to.
Teachers.
Attainment of pupils.

2.15 Differences in the teachers or the students might well have explained greater gains in arithmetic scores in the CAI, than in the non-CAI classes. For this reason, looking ahead to the possibility of using *statistical control* at the analysis stage, we undertook to obtain scores for each pupil on 'ability' (measured by IQ data already available in the school records), in addition to pre-test scores on the dependent variables. In view of the difficulty of measuring the 'quality' of teachers, we would only have information on their attitudes to CAI at three points during the year from the survey component (see paragraph 2.24 below). For each school we recorded its location as urban or rural; in addition, the ethnographic component was included to provide a much fuller description of schools.

statistical control

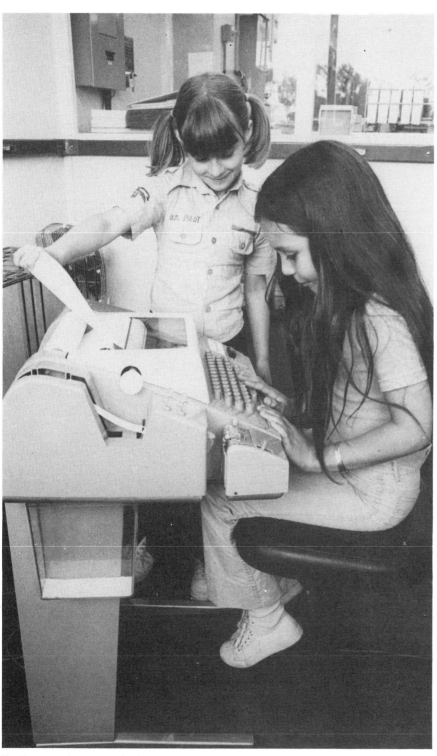

Pupils at work at a terminal

2.16   The ethnographers themselves had developed a number of 'generic problems' (Block 3, Part 5) in the course of a series of studies of classroom process (e.g. Smith and Geoffrey, 1968). These included: teacher decision making, dimensions of teacher–pupil relationships, classroom social structure and process, the behaviour of pupils in areas of poverty (urban and rural) and the effects of innovations on school organization. In the Eastern Kentucky study, they were interested in the impact of CAI on all these. We might say that they were interested in dependent variables different from those of the experimenters, and that some of these would be *unintended* features of the experience, over and above the (officially) *intended* effects of CAI.

2.17   In addition, the ethnographers aimed to describe the variation in teachers' use of CAI: the degree of integration with classroom activities, the use of print-out summaries of the students' work records, routines for sending children out of the classroom to the terminals, frequency of usage and so on. They were also interested in pupil behaviour at the terminals. Variations in these factors would crucially affect the meaning of the 'CAI treatment' for different groups of pupils. Hence, the significance of a retrospective comment from Lou Smith, one of the two ethnographers: 'We see the participant observation strand as an attempt to describe and conceptualize the nature of a very complex independent variable' (Smith, 1971).

2.18   Finally, knowledge of the distinctive cultural characteristics of Eastern Kentucky was essential for the aim of increasing the external validity of the *series* of studies of CAI that were being done. In addition, it was important to include an ethnographic component in the study in order, for example, to describe how certain schools and classrooms were allocated to CAI terminals, through various political (in the widest sense) processes and decisions within institutions like EKEDC (paragraph 2.11).

2.19   The two ethnographers spent 86 person-days in Eastern Kentucky. In the spring of the year before the full programme was to run, they made initial contacts with officials at EKEDC, personnel at the local university (which housed the feeder computer which was itself linked to the Stanford computer some 2000 miles away) and with superintendents of the co-operating districts. That summer they spent a week at the workshop for training the teachers selected to use CAI. From September to May 1968–69, they were in Eastern Kentucky at least once during each month, and visited each of the nine CAI schools at least twice.

2.20   Three schools were selected for especially intensive observation. The first was the 'laboratory school' at the local university, for a number of reasons: the town was a communications centre for the region, the feeder computer was housed at the university, and the school was expected to provide a variety of models of arithmetic teaching. The second was a school in a less cosmopolitan community far from the centre of communications, and where one teacher taught all the arithmetic. The third was chosen because it was a church school and because it was located in the same community as EKEDC; this allowed easier access to information about the overall project. Each of these schools was close to at least one 'country school', which allowed the researchers to compare urban and rural schools in the same district (Smith and Pohland, 1969a, p. 120).

2.21   In addition, the researchers made comparisons with the university school at Stanford, and with the CAI project in Mississippi, through visits of several days in each case.

Before you read on, note down an example of the sampling of each of the settings (schools), times, events and people in the discussion above (paragraphs 2.19–2.20).

2.22 The ethnographers' normal role was close to that of the 'complete observer' (see Block 3, Part 5, section 8). Yet, as members of the research team, they were identified with the CAI innovation and hence 'we found ourselves constantly drawn more into the participant role in the sense of "making the system go"' (Smith and Pohland, 1969a, p. 119). This indicates that, once fieldwork begins, there may be pressures against the researchers' maintaining the role(s) decided on at the design stage.

2.23 The survey component of the research aimed to study the possibilities of 'diffusion' of the innovation; for even if its implementation was successful in the sense of producing gains in test scores for CAI pupils, it would be unlikely to be implemented in other school systems, if teachers, pupils, or parents did not like it. Thus, the CEMREL researchers were particularly interested in changes of attitude over the period when CAI terminals were installed in the schools.

2.24 Attitude questionnaires were administered to *all* teachers in schools which had CAI classes at the beginning, the middle and the end of the school year. Those teachers who were not using CAI were included for comparison purposes, as well as to determine whether participating teachers were discussing CAI with colleagues.

2.25 One questionnaire was administered to the pupils in CAI classes at the middle of the school year. This aimed at finding how pupils' feelings about arithmetic had changed since using CAI, through questions such as: 'Do you like arithmetic more or less or the same since using the computer terminals?'.

2.26 Interviews were conducted at the middle of the year with what was originally intended to be a random sample of parents of pupils assigned to CAI in either the first or the second part of the year. However, the interviews took a great deal more time than expected. Hence the interviewers concentrated on those parents whose children had already been exposed to CAI, and on those who were most accessible.

Results and Interpretation

2.27 The main finding of the analysis of the achievement data was that effectively no differences were observed between CAI and non-CAI groups *within*

CAI classrooms. This was not surprising for the first six months of the study, since the CAI system was hardly working in some schools, and not at all in others. The lack of difference between CAI and non-CAI groups for the second six months was more surprising; an explanation for this is provided by the ethnographic results (paragraph 2.33 below).

2.28 For the quasi-experiment, after *statistical control* for differences in pupils' pre-test scores, there were statistically significant differences[3] between the CAI classes (i.e. the CAI plus non-CAI groups) and the non-CAI classes for the arithmetic 'applications' variable in both semesters and for the 'computation' and 'concepts' variable in the second semester (see paragraph 2.9). However, this result may be due, not to CAI, but to the influence of rival factors, such as differences in teachers across the CAI and non-CAI classes (which were not established by randomization). There were found to be no differences in gains in achievement score between high and low 'ability' (IQ) groups.

2.29 For the results of the survey component, we begin with the teachers' questionnaire. The main finding was that teachers' favourability towards CAI *decreased* over the year. This decrease appears to be only slight when we compare the level of favourability expressed (on a five-point scale) in the September, January and May questionnaires; however, non-response made these comparisons difficult: only about two-thirds of the 119 teachers in the nine CAI schools answered the September questionnaire, and only one-third answered all three. To cope with this, the researchers asked the teachers in January to say how their attitudes to CAI had changed since September: a greater proportion of teachers of CAI classes than of teachers of non-CAI classes (58 per cent as against 44 per cent) reported that their attitudes had become less favourable – presumably as a result of the technical difficulties with the system, though in addition a few teachers did not like the division of their (CAI) class into CAI and non-CAI groups (Rigsby and McIntire, 1969, p. 75).

2.30 Among the pupils, 70 per cent reported that they 'liked very much using the computer terminal for arithmetic'; 22 per cent 'liked it OK'; and 7 per cent 'didn't like it'. This result surprised many teachers, in view of the reactions of frustration and disgust they had observed among the pupils when the terminals did not work properly. The researchers had also asked the pupils to say whether the other children in their classes liked using the terminal; these proportions were lower (57, 38 and 5 per cent respectively) than the self-report questions. One teacher suggested the reason might be that, although her pupils 'answered all questions honestly . . . they were eager to please' (Rigsby and McIntire, 1969, p. 75).

2.31 As indicated above (paragraph 2.26) only a small number of parents were interviewed because of the time and travel involved for each interview, and the interviewers concentrated on those who were most accessible: basically those who lived in the two or three towns in the area, rather than those in the rural areas. This resulted in a response rate of 63 per cent (25 out of 40). The researchers point out that this tends to imply that the sample was better educated and of a higher socio-economic status than the general population of Eastern Kentucky (Rigsby and McIntire, 1969, p. 68). Eighteen of the twenty-five parents were in favour of CAI being used the following year for arithmetic questions, but only fourteen answered that they would favour a tax increase if CAI had to be paid for

---

[3]*Statistically significant differences are differences which are too large to have arisen 'by chance' – that is, simply as a result of variation due to sampling, between the two groups being compared. See Block 3, Part 4 for a discussion of sampling variation, and Block 6 for a discussion of statistical tests of significance.*

with local funds – and the interviewers indicated that many parents were extremely hesitant about answering this question.

2.32 We can show how problems of external population validity can be dealt with even when a random sample (Block 3, Part 4) is impossible, or when practical difficulties (e.g. of accessibility and/or non-response as in this study) have vitiated the original randomness of the sample. The researchers used their knowledge of the setting and the population to assess the ways in which the sample was unlikely to be representative, and the importance of this. Eighteen of the twenty-five parents in the sample (72 per cent) were middle class; this was a much higher percentage than in the region as a whole (Rigsby and McIntire, 1969, p. 60). Since, *within* the sample, parents with white collar or professional jobs were slightly more inclined to answer 'yes' to local tax support for CAI than working-class people, we should allow for the over-representation of the former when we seek to generalize the results of this question *beyond* the sample.[4]

2.33 The ethnographers described various facets of life in Eastern Kentucky; I cannot present the details of their description here, but they were summarized under the broad concept of 'cultural isolation' (Smith and Pohland, 1969b, p. 19). Their holistic approach included an account of the impact of the cut of federal government funds on the project, notably the decision to have one rather than two terminals in each CAI school. Their description of the nature and effect of the many system breakdowns helped to explain the lack of difference between CAI and non-CAI groups, especially in the first semester. The lack of difference between the two groups in the second semester (when the system was working better) can perhaps be explained by the teachers providing a classroom setting that tended to minimize the differences between the CAI and the non-CAI halves of the class. The ethnographers noted differences in teacher utilization of CAI that ranged from 'no observable attempt at integration to constructing the entire year's mathematics program around it' (Smith and Pohland, 1969b, p. 30). In terms of pupil utilization, there was a great deal of enthusiasm, as expected, and a tendency towards group activity around the terminals, an unexpected consequence. This included fighting to get on to the terminals, and competition as to who could finish an exercise in the least time, and as to who could get the highest proportion of answers correct, though correctness seemed to be less important than speed (Smith and Pohland, 1969b).

2.34 Ethnographic research not only produces a meaningful account of the nature of the independent variable and the variety of its effects; it also generates certain *anecdotes*, which, retrospectively at least, can seem as indicative of the way the various (explanatory) factors were experienced and interpreted by the actors in the setting. For example, we have indicated that technical breakdowns and difficulties caused a great deal of frustration to the teachers and pupils using CAI; one little girl, to whom the terminal printed out 'CRY AGAIN' (instead of 'TRY AGAIN') reported to her teacher 'Oh, Mrs Martin, I could just cry again and again' (quoted in Smith and Pohland, 1969b, p. 17). Another anecdote related by the ethnographers on the team was 'Roger's tale':

> According to the teachers, his reputation at the school had been one of a mentally handicapped child mixed with a large dose of cantankerousness and laziness. . . . The story, at any rate, is that rather than doing just one lesson at the terminals, Roger stayed at the terminals until he had completed

---

[4]*This process of allowing for differences in certain characteristics (here, social class composition) between the sample and the population is a form of statistical control, called 'standardization' by Kish (1959, p. 329). It should be distinguished from standardization of subjects at the design stage (see Part 2, paragraph 3.4).*

four of them. He was bound and determined to sit there until he had got 100 per cent on one of the drills and on the fourth try he did. He ended up with a print-out about five feet long that he displayed very proudly. The teachers refused to believe that he had done it all by himself . . . (field notes 5 December 1968) . . . we have had a long-standing commitment to the educational process . . . that will 'turn kids on' and make learning an exciting and stimulating adventure. CAI was such an experience for Roger. From what we could infer, Roger was a potential drop-out who was 'saved' in the best sense of the word. For Roger, and others like him, CAI was well worth the cost. (Smith and Pohland, 1969b, pp. 46–8)

2.35 The ethnographers summarized the results of their components of the research in this way:

In a sense we were questioning the formal doctrine of CAI, seeking to discover the stimulus configurations which in a complex way were responsible for the concentration, enthusiasm, attention, and anxiety we observed . . . CAI had considerable social significance. Overt manifestations of this were in the group rather than individual activities frequently observed at the teletypes and the varying forms of competition that developed . . . we began to see CAI not as a simple and straightforward drill routine, but as a complex of physical, social, emotional, and cognitive behaviours inextricably intertwined, and shaped both by administrative routines and norms of the particular schools and classrooms. For us all of these elements were combined in a unique yet general way in Roger's tale. (Smith and Pohland, 1969b, p. 48)

2.36 We can sum up the overall results of the installation of CAI and the evaluation study as follows:

(a)   The pupils appeared to benefit from the CAI drill, as indicated by greater gains in scores on computation, concepts, and applications in the CAI classrooms, as compared with the non-CAI classrooms; however, only some of these differences were statistically significant and internal validity was a problem (paragraph 2.28).

(b)   They also benefited in terms of greater academic involvement in general and with mathematics in particular. Further, they were exposed to an educational innovation in the form of new technology, with strengths and weaknesses alike.

(c)   The teachers benefited by having the opportunity to work with a new mode of teaching; though a number did not like the division of their classes into CAI and non-CAI groups. In addition, they were brought together with other teachers for an intensive workshop in connection with the implementation of CAI and course planning related to it.

(d)   On the other hand, the frequent technical failures brought frustration to pupils and teachers alike. This no doubt contributed to the less favourable attitudes among teachers, especially at the end of the first semester.

(e)   The region benefited, first in the educational sphere where local staff learned to work together across district boundaries to facilitate the introduction of CAI. Second, the telephone communication in the region was improved (since telephone lines were needed to connect the terminals in each school with the local feeder computer, which was in turn connected with the one at Stanford University).

(f)   Finally, the study documented the effect of technical complexity on the acceptance of an innovation such as CAI in a rural area like Eastern Kentucky. In addition, it pointed to the importance of economic costs for the possibilities of its adoption and diffusion (Russell, 1969, p. 107).

2.37   Besides its substantive and social importance, the study has also made a contribution to methodological discussions, particularly to do with the role of the ethnographic style in policy research, and with possibilities for combining the three styles of research.

> Perhaps the most significant feature of the CEMREL Evaluation Model is the separation and integration of the three different perspectives (i.e. styles) in evaluating CAI. Where the perspectives converge on a situation and produce data that are mutually reinforcing, the resulting conclusions have increased credibility and increased validity. In cases where the different perspectives converge on the same situation and the resulting data are mutually contradictory, there is even greater value in the results. Under such circumstances, apparently valid conclusions are seen to be invalid and apparently credible statements are seen to be not so credible. It is under such circumstances that the knowledge base increases or becomes firmer as a result of the evaluation activities. (Russell, 1969, p. 11)

3   Summary

3.1   Part 6 began by developing a rough check-list of decisions to be made at various stages of research in each of the three styles (based on Parts 2, 3, 4 and 5). I then attempted to compare the three styles of research in terms of their methodological commitments. We saw that each style tends to emphasize some of those methodological problems we have been discussing in the course and to play down others. Particular studies also differ in terms of the conceptual, political and ethical commitments of the researchers, though it is harder to differentiate the styles in these latter terms. I discussed the role of the various commitments in making design decisions and illustrated trade-offs between, for example, resource constraints and methodological commitments, in certain decisions.

3.2   Finally, I described in detail the design of a study to evaluate computer-assisted instruction in primary schools in Eastern Kentucky in 1967–69. This study used all three styles of research in order to cope with certain methodological problems, in the context of various commitments and constraints.

Objectives

By the end of Part 6 you should be able to:

1   Compile a list of decisions and activities involved in research design in each of the styles of research, as outlined in earlier Parts of this Block (section 1).

2   Compare the three styles in terms of their major methodological 'commitments' (section 1).

3   Illustrate conceptual, political and ethical commitments, and resource constraints in research (section 1).

4   Identify decisions made on methodological, ethical, political and resource grounds in a given study, and to illustrate trade-offs between these criteria (sections 1 and 2).

5   Analyse the ways in which a given research design coped with the various methodological problems discussed in the course so far (section 2).

Appendix: Methodological Commitments of the Three Styles

Aspect	Experimental	Survey	Ethnographic
(a) Relative emphasis (within each style) on control, representation and description	A great deal on control; less on representation and description of the setting; sometimes more on description of 'explanatory variables' (treatments and 'measuring instruments') (Block 3, Part 2)	A great deal on representation; no emphasis on control, if 'descriptive'; more, if explanatory; little emphasis on description of setting of interview; sometimes description of interview schedule but little attention to unwritten and especially non-verbal elements of interaction (Block 3, Part 3)	A great deal on description of the setting (Block 3, Part 5, sections 3–5) and events; emphasis on control and representation depends on the stage of research and progressive focusing (Block 3, Part 5, section 2)
(b) Methods of control	'Physical' control: random allocation to treatment groups and standardization of laboratory conditions (see also other methods discussed in Block 3, Part 2, section 3)	'Statistical' control or statistical adjustment; sometimes by time series or repeated contact designs (Block 3, Part 3, section 2)	The comparative method: theoretical sampling in the discovery stage and analytic induction in later stages (Block 3, Part 5, section 2)
(c) Methods of representation	Individuals – sometimes probability sampling, often representative samples are *assumed*; settings and events – replication of the study at different times or places, with different version of treatment or dependent variable	Individuals – usually probability sampling; sometimes sampling of places (via cluster sampling e.g. Plowden); sampling of times done in time series and repeated contact designs	Individuals, time and events – 'theoretical sampling' in the discovery stage and 'methodical sampling' in later stages (Block 3, Part 5, sections 2 and 9); setting – usually chosen purposively (Block 3, Part 5, section 3)
(d) Relative concern with internal and external validity	Properly designed laboratory experiments can be strong on internal validity but weak on external validity, because of the artificiality (lack of 'naturalism') of the conditions under which they are carried out and the (frequent) lack of attention to sampling. Note that the first of these two limitations is *necessary* (a laboratory study *must* be *artificial*) whereas the second is *contingent* (experimenters could pay more attention to sampling issues than they generally do; see Block 3, Part 2). Surveys can be much stronger in terms of population validity and perhaps ecological validity (depending on where, how and by whom the interview is conducted). However, of necessity, they are weaker than experiments on internal validity; that is, on control of rival hypotheses that might explain the findings for that particular research context; yet 'the advantages of experiments over surveys in permitting better control are only relative, not absolute' (Kish, 1959).		

One of the strengths of ethnographic research is its emphasis on naturalism, process, and holism (Block 3, Part 5, section 1); this provides the basis for greater *ecological* validity (generalizing to other settings, and so on): it is less concerned with population validity. Through its commitment to understanding and multiple perspectives, it is also concerned with internal validity in situations where the alternative explanatory hypotheses have to do with different possible interpretations by the actors participating in the study.

Answers to Self-assessment Questions

SAQ 1

(a)   People would be likely to volunteer:
(i)   if they wanted or needed $4 for an hour's 'work'; and/or
(ii)   if they were interested in psychological research; but
(iii)   only if they were free during the hours that the experiment was being conducted; and
(iv)   only if they saw the adverts for the experiment (or were told about it by their friends).

Excluded would be richer people, busy people, people sceptical of the value of psychological experiments and people who did not know about the experiment. People with characteristic (ii) might well be unusually deferent to a psychologist. If this were so, and if the experiment recruited a relatively high proportion of such people, the sample of volunteers would tend to be more obedient to a psychologist than would the *general population* (which we have inferred for Milgram was all human beings (Block 3, Part 1, paragraph 1.12)). If that were the case (how could we check this? see the answer to SAQ 2 below) there would be no problems with external (population) validity.

(b)   If we increase the payment for an hour's labour, we would expect more people to volunteer. This is based on general economic theories which predict that when a higher price is available for a good, there will be a greater supply of it. So on this reasoning (assuming that the economic theory is well-corroborated and holds true for this type of labour), the sample recruited on this basis ($8 per hour) would *tend to be* more representative of the general propulation. This would improve the external validity of the study. However, if resources were held constant, the sample could only be half the size. Here we have a trade-off between the size of a sample and the elimination of bias. Psychologists, however, would wonder about *cognitive dissonance* (Crowle, 1976, p. 161): potential volunteers **cognitive dissonance** might both wish to participate, yet wonder if there was a 'catch' – if $8 per hour seemed to them to be an abnormally high wage. This quandary might lead some to be suspicious and hence to decline to volunteer. In this case, the higher wage would actually increase the bias of the sample.

SAQ 2

The above characteristics, (i) and perhaps (iii) might suggest that the sample might be less well-educated than the general population. However, when we *check* this with the observed characteristics of Milgram's sample we find that only 1 person in about 300 had not finished high school (secondary school)! (Milgram, 1974, p. 16). We could conclude that it is unlikely that the sample has a lower educational level than that of the American population. To say this we could use our everyday knowledge about American educational levels or we could consult statistical sources for that country.

SAQ 3

Figure 3　CAI evaluation design

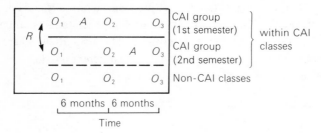

6 months 6 months

Time

References

ARGYRIS, C. (1952) 'Diagnosing defences against the outsider', *Journal of Social Issues*, Vol. 8, No. 3, pp. 24–34, reprinted in McCall, G. C. and Simmons, J. L. (eds) (1969) *Issues in participant observation: a text and reader*, Reading, Mass., Addison-Wesley, pp. 115–25.

BYNNER, J. and STRIBLEY, K. M. (eds) (1979) *Social research: principles and procedures*, London, Longman/The Open University Press. (Course Reader.)

CAMPBELL, D. T. (1969) 'Reforms as experiments', *American Psychologist*, Vol. 24, pp. 409–29, reprinted in Bynner, J. and Stribley, K. M. (eds) (1979) Ch. 9.

CROWLE, A. J. (1976) 'The deceptive language of the laboratory', in Harré, R. (ed.) *Life sentences: aspects of the social role of language*, London, John Wiley, pp. 160–74.

LACEY, C. (1970) *Hightown Grammar*, Manchester, University of Manchester Press.

KISH, L. (1959) 'Some statistical problems in research design', *American Sociological Review*, Vol. 24 (June), pp. 328–38, reprinted in Bynner, J. and Stribley, K. M. (eds) (1979) Ch. 8. (Set Reading.)

MILGRAM, S. (1974) *Obedience to authority: an experimental view*, London, Tavistock.

MARSH, C. (1979) 'Opinion polls: social science or political manoeuvre?', in Irvine, J., Miles, I. and Evans, J. *Demystifying social statistics*, London, Pluto Press.

RIGSBY, L. and McINTIRE, E. (1969) 'Attitudes toward computer-assisted instruction in nine southern Appalachian schools: a survey perspective', in Russell, H. H. (ed.) (1969) Ch. 3.

RUSSELL, H. H. (ed.) (1969) *Evaluation of computer-assisted instruction program*, St Louis, CEMREL.

RUSSELL, H. H. and EVANS, J. T. (1969) 'Student achievement in CAI program', in Russell, H. H. (ed.) (1969) Ch. 4.

SJOBERG, G. and NETT, R. (1968) *Methodology for social research*, New York, Harper and Row.

SMITH, H. W. (1975) *Strategies of social research: the methodological imagination*, New York, Harper and Row. (Set Book.)

SMITH, L. M. (1971) 'Integrating participant observation into broader evaluation strategies', American Educational Research Association, Symposium on Participant Observation, 1971; reprinted in Hamilton, D. *et al* (eds) (1977) *Beyond the numbers game*, London, Macmillan.

SMITH, L. M. and GEOFFREY, W. (1968) *The complexities of an urban classroom: an analysis toward a general theory of teaching*, New York, Holt Rinehart and Winston.

SMITH, L. M. and POHLAND, P. A. (1969a) 'CAI fieldwork methodology: grounded theory and educational ethnography', in Russell, H. H. (ed.) (1969) Appendix I.

SMITH, L. M. and POHLAND, P. A. (1969b) 'Participant observation of the CAI program', in Russell, H. H. (ed.) (1969) Ch. 2.

SUPPES, P., JERMAN, M. and BRIAN, D. (1968) *Computer-assisted instruction: Stanford's 1965–66 arithmetic program*, New York, Academic Press.

Acknowledgements for Parts 4, 5 and 6

Grateful acknowledgement is made to the following for permission to reproduce material in these Parts of this Block:

Part 4:   Cartoons on pp. 3 and 35 from H. Hargreaves, *The bird set*, Macmillan and Co.; Table 1 from *A million random digits with 100 000 normal deviates*, Macmillan Publishing Co., New York, reproduced by permission of the Rand Corporation; Table 2 from Hansen *et al, Sample survey methods and theory*, Vol. 1, John Wiley and Sons, 1953; Table 5 and table in Appendix A from *Statistics of Education – Universities*, Vol. 6, 1968, reproduced by permission of the Controller of HMSO; Figure 4 from Hansen *et al*, 1953, *op. cit.*

Part 5:   p. 41 *The Observer;* Figure 1 from B. H. Junker, *Field work*, University of Chicago Press, 1960; p. 46 Bildarchiv Preussischer Kulturbesitz (Weber); p. 46 Michael Joseph (Mead); p. 48 courtesy of T. and R. Annan and Sons Ltd.; p. 49 Pitt Rivers Museum; p. 51 (top) *The Observer*/Michael Peto, (bottom) Chris Schwarz; p. 61 (bottom) British Gas, (top) Grand Metropolitan Hotels; p. 65 Barnaby Picture Library; p. 69 *The Observer*.

DE304   Research Methods in Education and the Social Sciences

Block Co-ordinators

Block 1 M. J. Wilson, Block 2 Robert Peacock, Block 3 Jeff Evans and John Bynner, Block 4 John Bynner,
Block 5 John Bynner, Block 6 M. J. Wilson, Block 7 Peter Coxhead and M. J. Wilson, Block 8 R. J. Sapsford